The Complete Book of Figure Skating

Carole Shulman

Executive Director,
Professional Skaters Association

Human Kinetics

Library of Congress Cataloging-in-Publication Data

Shulman, Carole, 1940-
    The complete book of figure skating / Carole Shulman.
        p.   cm.
    Includes index.
    ISBN 0-7360-3548-6
    1. Skating.   I. Title.
    GV850.4   .S49   2001
    796.91'2--dc21

2001026394

ISBN: 0-7360-3548-6

Developmental Editor: Laura Hambly; **Assistant Editor**: Kim Thoren; **Copyeditor**: Karen L. Marker; **Proofreader**: Joanna Hatzopoulos Portman; **Indexer**: Joan Griffitts; **Permission Manager**: Toni Harte; **Graphic Designer**: Nancy Rasmus; **Graphic Artist**: Sandra Meier; **Photo Manager**: Tom Roberts; **Cover Designer**: Keith Blomberg; **Photographer (cover)**: Eddy LeMaistre; **Photographer (interior)**: Tom Roberts, unless otherwise noted; **Art Manager**: Carl Johnson; **Illustrator**: Accurate Art; **Printer**: Versa Press

Human Kinetics books are available at special discounts for bulk purchase. Special editions or book excerpts can also be created to specification. For details, contact the Special Sales Manager at Human Kinetics.

Printed in the United States of America

10   9   8   7   6   5   4   3   2   1

Human Kinetics
Web site: www.humankinetics.com

United States: Human Kinetics
P.O. Box 5076
Champaign, IL 61825-5076
800-747-4457
e-mail: humank@hkusa.com

Canada: Human Kinetics
475 Devonshire Road Unit 100
Windsor, ON N8Y 2L5
800-465-7301 (in Canada only)
e-mail: orders@hkcanada.com

Europe: Human Kinetics
Units C2/C3 Wira Business Park
West Park Ring Road
Leeds LS16 6EB, United Kingdom
+44 (0) 113 278 1708
e-mail: hk@hkeurope.com

Australia: Human Kinetics
57A Price Avenue
Lower Mitcham, South Australia 5062
08 8277 1555
e-mail: liahka@senet.com.au

New Zealand: Human Kinetics
P.O. Box 105-231, Auckland Central
09-523-3462
e-mail: hkp@ihug.co.nz

To David, my perfect partner on the ice and off.

contents

Part I Essentials

Part II Techniques

foreword

More than 20 years have passed since the first controlled study was conducted on the physiological, psychological, and nutritional factors involved in developing the figure skater as an athlete. Prior to that time, the development and advancement of figure skating skills had been the responsibility of the skater and coach.

As the scientific community became more alert to the needs and inherent dangers of our sport's rapid advancement, ice skating organizations began establishing recommended parameters to guide figure skaters in becoming the healthiest, strongest, soundest athletes in the history of the sport. At the same time, a generation of coaches, athletes, and officials has contributed an immeasurable amount of time and effort to assure that this ever-changing and amazingly beautiful sport is both scientifically and technically guarded.

Understanding the training methods and exercises behind sound technique and execution is vital to advancement in the sport. At long last, that essential information has been compiled and formatted in the most comprehensive book ever written on figure skating. This book is a guide to all who wish to pursue the sport of figure skating to their highest potential. It establishes the basis around which coach and pupil may imprint their own personal signature on the sport.

Carole Shulman presents the finest and most complete work ever prepared on skating: a masterful arrangement of detail and progression along the path of fundamental development.

Donald Laws
Former president of the Professional Skaters Association
and coach of 1984 Olympic gold-medal winner Scott Hamilton.

preface

Many instructional books have been written about figure skating. Some are very good. Others are outdated. None, however, are complete. *The Complete Book of Figure Skating* finally fills that void. Written for skaters and coaches, it is the most comprehensive, up-to-date book ever written on skating. It covers skills done in all disciplines, including singles, pairs, ice dancing, and synchronized team skating.

In December of 1984 I became the executive director of the Professional Skaters Association (PSA), then called the Professional Skaters Guild of America (PSGA). Education and training for coaches were top priority on the list of activities included in my job description. The task did not intimidate me, for I knew that I could organize and supervise educational seminars. What is truly amazing is that throughout the 62-year history of this organization, we never had, or even thought of having, a complete textbook on skating.

We thought we were becoming very good at sharing information at annual seminars and conferences, but we didn't want to "tell it all" because then anyone would be able to coach. We understood that some parents believed they could coach their own children, and if their coaching worked for their children, they certainly could teach others. After all, coaching isn't work, it's fun!

I look back on the history of figure skating and muse that our sport is not unlike the ancient civilizations. There was no written communication, only word of mouth passed from one generation to another. In skating, the coach teaches the student and the student eventually becomes the coach. That student teaches future students and on and on the knowledge is passed along. Only recently, with understanding gained from sport scientists, have we learned that our technique is good. Our methods are correct and our results are proven by the number of successful U.S. skaters who stand on the Olympic podium each quadrennium. But most coaches don't understand why they teach the way they do. They just know it works. For a hundred years coaches have taught biomechanics without knowing the meaning of the word.

Coaches and skaters now have a resource to turn to for learning those same techniques and training methods that have proven so successful in the past. In *The Complete Book of Figure Skating,* instruction starts at the beginning—sitting on the ice and then learning to move across the frozen surface, at first timidly but eventually with speed, style, and grace. The chapters build in difficulty, covering steps, spins, jumps, and lifts. From stopping to spinning to quad jumps, each skill builds on the previous skills as this complete manual guides you from the basics to advanced techniques.

This book is divided into three parts. Part I covers the essentials, including descriptions of each of the skating disciplines, information on selecting proper equipment, and advice on off-ice conditioning and nutrition. Part II describes the proper technique for more than 100 skills, including stops, stroking skills, freestyle moves, turns and footwork (including ice dancing techniques), spins, jumps, and pair skating techniques. In these chapters, the skills are presented progressively from beginning to advanced levels of expertise. Each skill is described with introductory or preparatory steps followed by a detailed technical explanation designed to enhance understanding and training. Most skills conclude with a tip or a teaching exercise that can be performed either off the ice or at the rink barrier. The tips and exercises focus on the major component of the skill, which is often the most difficult concept to understand and master. Teaching Tips are addressed to coaches, while Training Tips are addressed to skaters. Finally, part III contains information on performances. You'll learn the ins and outs of creating a program, including information on music, choreography, and costumes. You'll also find tips on how to perfect skills and score high marks from the judges.

Whether you're a skater looking to improve your technique or an instructor looking for innovative coaching methods, this book will help you achieve your goal.

acknowledgments

Tantamount to the success of this book is the help I have received from friends and colleagues. Not a single person that I asked for help turned me down. I am grateful to Jay Freeman, Kim Goss, Sandy Lamb, Tom Zakrajsek, Don Laws, Kathy Casey, my daughter Tracy Jackson, and Ann-Margreth Frei-Hall.

Special thanks to the skaters who appear in the photographs: Jessica Horner, Marisa Mitchell, Tiffany Phan, Alison Hoyer, Emily Hoyer, Paul Wood, Laura McKusick, Sarah Berquist, Aisling Linehan, and Andrew Goldman.

I am also grateful to all my former coaches, to my father, and especially my mother, who got me started in figure skating and who faithfully chauffeured me back and forth to the rink, made my costumes, and convinced Dad that this was all worthwhile. Without Mom I would never have started or, more important, continued.

There are two men in my life who deserve special credit. Robert Ogilvie, an author and former coach of mine, deserves a word of thanks for his painstaking efforts in reviewing every word of the technical portions of this text. His knowledge and love of skating are profound and quite simply awesome. We spent many hours on the phone having philosophical discussions on the technique and trends of our sport. The man is delightful!

The other man is my husband, who is my life encourager. With the support he has given me over the years, I have grown and exceeded even my own goals and expectations. I am because he is.

The exercise of writing this book has taught me an important lesson: When done well, coaching is work. When work is done well, it looks effortless and it is fun!

introduction: the sport of beauty and athleticism

The exact who, where, and when of the origins of skating will never be known for certain. Early carvings indicate that skating was practiced in the Scandinavian countries almost 1600 years ago, and archeological evidence shows that skating dates back to the earliest known period of human culture. Early people strapped the rib bones of oxen or the shank bones of elk and reindeer to their feet and propelled themselves across the ice with poles. The word *skate* is derived from the old German word *schake*, meaning shank, or leg bone, similar to *scatch* in old English and *schaat* in Flemish.

This type of skate has been found in many parts of Europe—Norway, Switzerland, Denmark, Sweden, and even England. One pair made from the cannon bone of a horse was found bound to the skeleton of a Stone Age man discovered in Holland. Another set, made of walrus teeth, was found in Sweden. This new invention remained virtually unchanged until about the 14th century, when waxed wood replaced bone.

The Dutch played a significant role in the history of skating. In fact, skating is probably the only sport to have its own saint. A 16-year-old Dutch girl, born in 1380, became an invalid after a fall while skating. Many miracles were attributed to her before her death in 1433. Saint Ludwina (or Ludwila) was canonized in 1890 by the Roman Catholic Church and named patron saint of skating in 1944.

The Dutch are also credited with the development of the narrow metal blade—by accident. No one is quite sure exactly when the metal blade was introduced, but legend has it that a traveler in Holland asked a blacksmith to make a pair of blades. The blacksmith misunderstood the instructions and made the skates with a narrow surface. This new, thin blade gave more stability and maneuverability, and the "mistake" soon spread the popularity of skating throughout Europe as well as in America.

Some of the Stuarts who had fled to Holland during the Cromwell Royal reign later returned to Britain, bringing with them the new sport. While the Dutch and Scandinavians became keen racers along canals and lakes, the British began to develop an organized artistic and recreational approach to ice skating, to the extent that the first skating club was founded in Edinburgh in 1742, and the first instructional book, *A Treatise on Skating* by Robert Jones, was published in 1772. In it, Jones acknowledges the beginnings of skating for more than the sake of mere recreation or transportation. "No motion can be more happily imagined for setting off an elegant figure to advantage, nor does the minuet itself afford half the opportunity of displaying a pretty foot. . . ."

Grooves, or flutes, began appearing in the skates about this time, along with development skills that used the blades' edges. The Dutch Roll is simply another name for what we consider today to be the natural method of skating on inside and outside edges. Though the style may have come from the Dutch, it was Henry Boswell, an Englishman, who by 1837 had developed an improved blade for figure skating, shorter in the front and longer in the back, leading to the intricate tracings of figures.

English soldiers and immigrants brought the sport to America. As the principal city of the new world, Philadelphia was also the site of the founding of the first club in 1849 for "the purpose of improvement, pleasure, companionship, and safety of skaters." Eleven years later the club took its present name, the Philadelphia Skating Club and Humane Society, having joined with the society to patrol the Schuylkill River and rescue unfortunate skaters who had fallen through the ice. The club was one of the charter members of the United States Figure Skating Association when it was founded in 1921.

Two of the greatest advancements in the development of the skate were the invention of a clamp-on skate, developed about 1848, and the development of a blade permanently attached to the boot. These advances were responsible for bringing skating to the general public. By the time of the Civil War more than 200 different skate blades were on the market.

It was also about that time that skating techniques were improved and Jackson Haines, a little-known American ballet master, thrilled spectators with his daring combination of skating and dance. In the United States, where the accepted rigid style of figure skating was established, Haines' free expressive movements were frowned upon, although he won the title of U.S. Champion in 1863. He left the United States for Vienna, where he adapted waltzes and dances to ice. His free style of skating was hailed throughout Europe and was the forerunner of today's sport and entertainment.

The International Skating Union (ISU) was formed in Holland in 1892 at a meeting attended by representatives from six countries. Its first world figure skating championships were held in St. Petersburg in 1896, marking the beginning of official world competition. Olympic competition followed in 1908.

Possibly the greatest innovation, next to the skate itself, was the ability to make artificially frozen ice. There had been experiments as early as 1812, but in 1876 an Englishman named W.A. Parker made the first artificial ice in a surface large enough to skate on—24 feet wide by 40 feet long. The rink was not open to the public but reserved for noblemen. Within several years artificial surfaces began to appear throughout the world, offering the possibility of ice skating as a year-round sport for everyone to enjoy.

Figure skating was well on its way. The modern skate blade had been invented, artificial ice was being made, an international organization had been created, and the first world championship had been held. Next came the heroes and heroines of the sport. In the years to come, a number of skating stars emerged to help shape the sport into what it is today. Among these are Axel Paulsen, who brought us the Axel jump in 1882; Ulrich Salchow, who invented the Salchow in 1910; Madge Syers, who paved the way for women in competition; Sonja Henie, who increased the sport's popularity; and Dick Button, who brought skating to a new level of athleticism.

© EMPICS/Scanpix

Sonja Henie, shown here at the 1928 Winter Olympics in St. Moritz, made a lasting impact on both the popularity and technique of figure skating.

Gone are the days when figures were skated before you could qualify for freestyle. In fact, gone are figures all together. Gone are the bent knees, the long skirts for women, the formal wear for men, and the formality of hats and gloves. Present today are quads, designer costumes, scientific analysis, and high-tech training.

part I

Essentials

chapter 1
Skating Disciplines

Figure skating is a wonderful and gratifying sport. It is fun to learn and it is glorious, even inspirational, to watch. Figure skating requires the training and athleticism of any rigorous sport along with the grace and agility of a ballerina, the speed of a sprinter, the creativity of an artist, and the talent of an entertainer.

The basic skills in skating are acquired in either group or private lessons, but in the beginning skating is a self-centered endeavor. When you first learn to skate, you cannot rely on a team, a coach, or a mentor. You must learn the skills and stand on your own merit. Later, you may consider a dance or pair partner, or you may join a synchronized team, an exciting and quickly growing segment of figure skating. Or you may decide to branch out and rechannel your talent and energy by spreading the joy and thrill of skating to others—a most rewarding experience! Whether you want to perfect your own skating technique or be a more effective coach to others, this book will help you get the most out of your practice sessions so that you can achieve your goals.

A skater's enjoyment and success in figure skating depends largely on the coach. For those readers who are learning to skate, this chapter explains ways to go about selecting a coach and highlights some of the qualities to look for in an instructor. This chapter also sheds light on the different challenges and rewards of each skating specialty. Whether you're a skater or a coach, compare your strengths and weaknesses to the demands of each discipline in order to select the one that's right for you. If you're a skater, remember that regardless of which specialty you choose you will need commitment, hard work, and practice to become an expert on the ice! If you're a coach, pay close attention to the special duties and requirements for each discipline.

The Right Coach

Choosing the right coach is one of the most important decisions you can make in skating. If you begin with group lessons you may be assigned to a particular coach, and as you progress you will likely be rotated through several different coaches. This is a wonderful opportunity to sample a variety of personalities and teaching styles. If you are able to make your own selection, choose a coach who specializes in the area of your particular interest—for example, a dance coach, a singles coach, or a high- or low-level coach.

Choose someone you like and respect or whose reputation can be verified by others you know and trust. Investigate the coach's background and experience. Find out the answers to the following questions:

- Who was the coach's instructor?
- Where did the coach train?
- What credentials does the coach have, and what titles did he or she earn?
- What other students, past and present, has this person coached?
- Does the coach have a PSA rating?
- What are this person's coaching philosophies, and do they match your own?

It is not important that you seek an international-level coach unless you are interested in competing at an international level. It may be that your goals are to skate and enjoy the social experience. If so, it is important that you find a coach who will support your interests and help to fulfill your goals.

A coach will have a profound influence in your life. If you continue skating for many years, your coach becomes like a member of your family, shaping your goals and teaching discipline, respect, good sporting behavior, positive attitudes, and life skills along with skating technique.

Different Types of Skating

It's important for you to expose yourself to all types of skating so that you can specialize in what's right for you. Skating can be recreational or competitive, and it attracts individual skaters, dance and pair partners, and teams. One discipline is not better than the others; it's simply a question of what fits each skater and coach best.

Recreational Skating

As a recreational skater, you will participate primarily in group classes. This has many benefits. The cost is low, the social interaction is fun, and you can learn quickly from the strengths and the mistakes of others in the class.

As a recreational skating coach, you will have regular hours, lots of new people to meet, and little work outside the rink. The recreational coach is perhaps the most important factor in the development of the skater and customer satisfaction: If skaters enjoy their group lessons, they return to the rink over and over again. If you advance to a skating director or rink manager position, your hours, salary, responsibilities, and homework will increase.

Competitive Skating

If you are considering competitive skating, you must plan to spend many hours each day at the rink with only one or two days off each week. You may still continue with group lessons, but as you advance you will likely take more private lessons. You may go to the rink more than once a day, depending on the rink schedule. Plan on early morning or late evening hours, or both. Off-ice strength training and conditioning are mandatory, as are lessons in ballet, jazz, ballroom dancing, or gymnastics. You will spend hours evaluating and selecting music, plus many additional hours on the ice learning choreography for your programs. You will take tests and enter competitions, which can be stressful, expensive, and—in the case of failure—disappointing and maddening. Test sessions can also help to build character and discipline, but if the challenge and enjoyment do not outweigh the rewards, then this is not the area for you.

As a competitive skating coach, you will have to dedicate many hours to your profession. In addition to all the duties listed for the recreational coach, the competitive coach must plan training schedules, prepare periodization charts, know the proficiencies and competencies, and do a lot of traveling domestically and internationally. You can derive a very good income from this profession, but you won't be able to spend much time at home.

Pair Skating

You may enjoy watching pair skating and have a desire to try it yourself, or you may be searching for another avenue to go beyond singles skating. If you are interested in pairs, you must be strong (both partners), courageous (especially the lady), and

© Claus Andersen

The confidence and discipline of Michelle Kwan makes her the ideal singles skater.

compatible with your pair partner. You will be spending a lot of time together and you won't always get your own way. Skating with a partner requires precision, timing, and a healthy attitude!

As a singles or pairs coach, you will spend more off-ice time than a recreational coach in planning your lesson schedule, talking with students and parents, preparing music and programs, providing counseling, and traveling to other rinks to get enough ice time or to be with your students when they take tests. You will also receive more compensation than a recreational coach.

Singles Skating

If you're a skater who enjoys the individualism of skating alone and not having to share responsibilities—or having anyone else to blame when things don't go just right—then singles skating is for you. You must be self-motivated, disciplined, and confident, and you must enjoy the challenges of complex jumps and spins.

Ice Dancing

As an ice dancer, you must know how to skate edges better than skaters in either of the other disciplines. You will not be required to do the jumps and spins of singles skating, but you will have to adjust to a partner. Dance requires good rhythm, strong edges, and theatrical skills.

As an ice dancing coach, you will be much more involved as a skater than you would as a singles or pairs coach, although the interaction with students and parents and your responsibilities on and off the ice are very similar. It will be important for you to maintain your own high standard of skating. Because you will be expected to partner your students, you will always be in the public eye. You must know and be able to teach both the men's and ladies' steps for all the dances. You will be expected to take students through tests

© Bob Tringali/SportsChrome USA

Ice dancers, like Elizabeth Punsalan and Jerod Swallow, must have good rhythm, strong edges, and excellent theatrical skills.

and will need the proper attire. You should expect to teach late-evening hours as well as mornings.

Synchronized Team Skating

Team skating is growing. World synchronized championships are being held, and the skills are becoming challenging and complex. It is an exciting discipline in figure skating.

As a team skater, you will be able to participate at the recreational or competitive level. As with all group lessons, practice hours are set and penalties are imposed if you do not attend practices regularly. As your team becomes more skillful and wishes to attend more meets, your fund-raising activities will increase. The planning of schedules, test sessions, competitions, costuming, and trips is a team effort and requires the best interests of the group as a whole. Being a team skater has many benefits, but it also means that you will not have the independence of a singles, pair, or dance skater.

As a team coach, you will spend many hours off ice making or guiding the decisions that are made for the team. You will have the distinct responsibility of teaching a large group of skaters (12 to 24) to work together as a unit to perform intricate formations. You must possess technical skills as well as patience and reliability. With such a large group of people you must be prepared to meet both the mental and physical needs of each skater. You are responsible for the selection of the team, music, and costumes as well as for the scheduling of practice, choreography, competition selection, and supervision of training.

The team coach is also charged with the tasks of keeping the team focused, finding the strengths of individuals, using those strengths to better the team, and keeping the team excited. You must use the resources available to help you become a better coach. Because the team is your responsibility and rescheduling is a nightmare, you can never cancel practice. If the team is there, you must be there!

A parents' committee often helps in the planning and organization of the team. This committee is usually extremely helpful, but it requires additional hours to organize and administrate. It also requires patient listening skills to attend to all the ideas and complaints. Appointing a team manager or coordinator will help ease some of your responsibilities as team coach. The team manager is a volunteer parent who handles off-ice duties such as filling out forms, organizing the roster, and acting as liaison between the local organizing committee and the coach.

Summary

Choosing your discipline is somewhat like selecting a major in college. As a freshman you may determine a particular direction only to find that through exposure and new experiences your interests change entirely. By the time you graduate you may have chosen a path entirely different from the one in which you began. Likewise, you may discover that after you embark on your chosen skating path, new opportunities for growth and development come along. Years later, you may change once again. You may switch from one discipline to another, or you may find opportunities to expand to entirely different areas such as hockey power skating, or you may branch into management. As with any career, you must consider both lateral and upward growth to keep your mind alive and stimulated.

In addition to learning about skating disciplines and technique, you must have some basic knowledge about equipment to make you better informed. The next chapter addresses this subject.

chapter 2
Skates and Apparel

Equipment—particularly boots and blades—is an extremely important aspect of skating, especially at the competitive level. For example, the wrong pair of boots can affect balance and the ability to spin and jump. Coaches should have a working knowledge in this area so that they can provide sound advice to their skaters. Skaters should also be well informed to ensure that they buy equipment that fits well and meets their skating needs.

Boots and Blades

This section provides some insights into purchasing and maintaining equipment. Some areas where you should be knowledgeable include the following:

- Boot manufacturers and the general cost of boots
- Strength and stiffness of various models of boots
- How a boot should fit
- Boot maintenance
- When it's time for a new boot
- Various blade models, their uses, and performance features
- Blade mounting
- Blade maintenance

Part of the skating instructor's job is to recommend skates for students according to skaters' specific needs. This does not mean just telling the parents that their child has to have new skates and expecting them to go into the skate shop and buy a pair. It means that coaches should evaluate the entire situation, taking into consideration the parents' financial circumstances as well as the needs of each student. It's also important for skaters and their parents to do their homework, as they'll most likely be the ones spending their hard-earned money and will want to make sure they're investing it wisely.

Before deciding where to purchase skates, take the time to visit a few stores, such as the pro shop in your rink or a nearby sports shop. If you're a coach, check out the local shops to see who will work best with you and your students.

It is also a good idea to get to know each store's proprietor. Find out what selection of boots and blades the store offers and the prices. Learn what the proprietor recommends for different types of skaters and why. Find out who will be fitting the skates and who is most proficient at mounting and sharpening. If you're a coach, talk to the owner or manager about your preferences. Is the manager willing to call you if there are questions about specific selections? Can you be comfortable sending a student back to the shop for corrections? Be sure to leave your phone number and business card. If you send a pupil to buy new skates, always tell the parent to mention your name. As the proprietor of the skate shop becomes familiar with you and your preferences, he will be able to better advise your skater in making a selection. Chances are good that he will also give you, and your skaters, preferential treatment.

If there isn't a reliable vendor in your area, make some phone calls. There are many places in the United States that will accept a foot tracing and ball measurements to

The section on boots and blades was written by Tracy Jackson and edited by Carole Shulman. Jackson holds triple master ratings in figures, freestyle, group skating, and program administration and began coaching in 1987. She and her husband, Michael, sold and distributed boots and blades for many years. They reside in Denver, Colorado.

assess which boot is best. This generally only takes four to five days once the store receives the tracings. Once again, when you find the shop that will work with you long-distance, you should build a positive relationship with the proprietor. The management will respect that you won't settle for second best!

Selecting Skates

Advanced skaters usually buy boots and blades separately, whereas a beginning skater commonly has the boot and blade attached as a matched set.

Your prime consideration in choosing a skate is the shape of the foot. Some skaters have a boxy foot; others have a wide ball but narrow heel. If your two big toes point away from each another rather than being parallel when you stand with your feet side by side, you have the perfect Riedell foot! When the foot is boxy a Risport is appropriate, or for the young skater a Don Jackson Junior Competitor might be a better choice. You see, selecting skates is no different from choosing clothing. One brand of jeans may fit a size six, 120-pound person perfectly, whereas a different person who's the same size and weight may be better suited to a different brand simply because of differences in body shape. If you're a coach, be cautious about recommending just one or two types of skates; as you know, there are many different types of feet.

The chief consideration for beginners is finding boots that support them so that they can forget struggling with floppy ankles and get on with the fun and excitement of gliding on the ice. Unfortunately, you may find that while you want quality skates, you're not ready to spend a fortune to get them. This may be especially true if you've just seen a pair at a discount store for $29.95. In such cases you may have to do the best you can with what you have and look to upgrade at a later time.

Children

Perhaps you have seen tots or young children wearing molded boots. A molded boot is an inexpensive combination boot and blade that provides immediate support. However, molded boots do not allow children to "feel" the ice as they can in skating boots made of leather. Additionally, heavy boots can prevent young children from developing strength in the ankles. For skaters who plan to continue taking lessons, leather boots are recommended.

For some tots and young children, reconstructed boots—ones that have been used and rebuilt—could be a good way to start. Good used blades can usually be found. In some instances blades are already attached and the skates are a relatively inexpensive package. Skates of this type could be ideal for a child who is still in group lessons or just beginning private lessons. Reconstructed boots save the parent money yet put the child into better equipment.

Some skate shops do not rebuild boots; they merely carry used skates. There is a difference between reconstructed boots and used boots. Be sure you know which you are buying. Some used skates in the smaller sizes have been outgrown before they have been worn out, so they might be a good buy for a young child in beginning classes. Larger sized secondhand boots, however, are usually broken down and are not worth buying.

Most skate shops carry an inexpensive combination boot and blade. This can be a nice starter skate for a tot or young child. However, if the child shows promise, is taking private lessons, or is joining a club, a better quality boot and a separate blade is recommended.

If parents aren't quite ready to spend $90 to $120 on good leather boots and another $50 to $60 on blades, they could also consider renting skates. Then, once the skater asks to go skating more often and does well in classes, parents become more easily convinced that their child will stay in the sport and are more likely to purchase a good skate. As another possibility, a new product is the PSA boot and blade set, just introduced for around $135. The set features a Riedell leather boot and a Wilson blade that has slotted holes so that the blade can be adjusted to meet the skater's needs.

If a used boot is selected, make sure that it wasn't broken in incorrectly, or it will be no different from a vinyl boot. You can usually see this in the way the boot is creased. The best case for a used skate is when a skater is nearing the end of the group classes and is just starting basic jumps. If an expensive boot (originally priced at $300 to $400) can be found that is in good shape, it is probably a good deal. This gives the low-level skater a great boot at less than half the price. The boot that may not be strong enough for double Axels is generally perfect for single jumps. Many skaters have been turned off right from the beginning because of ill-fitting boots. A parent wouldn't enroll a child in piano lessons and give the child a Casio keyboard to practice on. The same principle applies to skaters as well!

Teenagers

By the time children become teenagers, their feet are usually too large for used equipment. Secondhand boots size six and larger are often too broken down to be a good buy. New skates are recommended.

The young teenager who is enthusiastic and is planning to take several lessons a week should definitely invest in a good pair of boots and blades. The young teenager who is mainly involved in activities outside of skating and who is planning to skate only once a week could do fine in an economically priced boot and blade.

The fully grown older teen who enjoys skating and plans to continue skating into adulthood should invest in a high-quality boot that will last for several years. If cost is an issue, begin with a less-expensive blade.

Adults

Adult skaters who plan to continue skating should buy high-quality boots. Adults will not outgrow their skates, so whatever they purchase will last a long time. Again, if cost is an issue, begin with a less expensive blade. In time it can be replaced with a blade of higher quality. When trying on different skates, keep in mind that too stiff or too heavy a boot can be too difficult for some adults to break in and can actually be detrimental to their skating.

Competitive Skaters

For serious skaters who are involved in tests and competitive skating, there are many things to think about when choosing skates. The skates must fit according to the skater's age, size, ability, strength, and style. The skater's goals and potential should also be taken into consideration. Some skaters are hard on boots and break them down quickly. They need strong boots. Others are light on the ice. They need boots that are supportive enough, yet still retain a graceful line.

Timing is important. Never buy new skates just before a competition or a test. You need sufficient time to break them in.

Skaters who are light on the ice, like Kristi Yamaguchi, need boots that give enough support but retain a graceful line.

Fitting and Caring for Boots

Whether you decide to buy skates that are new, used, or reconstructed, you'll want to ensure that the boots are fitted correctly. After all that work selecting the boots, it is also important to take proper care of them so that they don't break down prematurely. The following sections offer advice on fitting and maintaining boots.

Fitting Boots

When trying on boots, skaters should wear a pair of skating tights or the thinnest cotton sock possible. Many sporting goods stores fit skaters in a boot one or two sizes too big and then suggest wearing an extra pair of thick socks. Heavy socks restrict the skater's ability to maneuver the skate, however. It's comparable to skiing on a ski that is much too long.

Different brands of boots have different sizing. If you wear a size three shoe, a Riedell equivalent would be approximately a one and a SP-Teri would be a two. The sole of the boot on a Riedell is longer than any other boot, so if you're going from a Riedell to a SP-Teri and only moving up one size, you may not have to get a new blade. Chances are, it will fit perfectly! However, if your foot hasn't grown and you're changing from a SP-Teri to a Riedell, you will most definitely need a longer blade.

Never allow more than a half size of growing room in a boot, or the boot will break down very quickly (generally in less than four months). Keep in mind that the leather will give and expand slightly and may also stretch. A properly fitted boot should last, even with a major growth spurt, for at least six months. A normal growing period is 10 to 12 months. If the boot was fitted properly to begin with, the resale value will be much greater (generally 40 to 50 percent of the new price).

When determining if a boot fits properly, check the following:

- The heel to toe measurement must allow room for the toes to remain flat. Toes should be able to wiggle freely but not slide side to side.
- A snug fit in the heel should prevent any vertical movement. The skater's heel should not lift out of the heel cup.
- The counter (or arch support) must be long enough to support the inner longitudinal arch of the foot short of the ball joint.
- Put an unlaced boot on and slide the foot forward, touching the toe of the boot. If you can fit your finger behind the heel, it's too big.
- Never compensate length for width. It is better to get a wider boot than to increase the size if width is a problem.

Skaters are amazingly unaware when their boots become too small. Their feet seem to adapt to small boots by curling the toes and allowing the balls of the feet to squeeze together. This, of course, affects balance and the ability to perform to the skaters' maximum ability, particularly in spins and landing jumps.

The following warning signs suggest that a skater is growing out of a boot:

- Pain in the arch indicates that the counter is hitting the foot in the wrong place.
- Rocking to the toes on camel spins and rocking to the front of the blade on edge jumps denote a change in the skater's balance.
- Pressure across the ball of the foot indicates that the ball or widest part of the foot is pressing into the toe box area.
- Toes that are uncomfortable, particularly on toe jumps, are often the last indicator that a skater feels. By this time the boot is probably a full size too small.

A quick cure to consider for a boot that is getting too small is to take it to a boot or shoe repair shop and have it stretched. Remember that boots can be stretched no more than one-half to one full size in either length or width. Another possibility is to remove the innersole. Although the boot is rough to the touch without the innersole, most skaters do not seem to be disturbed by the stitching. If sensitivity is a problem, Dr. Scholl's foot pad can be used as a substitute. It is definitely thinner than an innersole, allowing more room. Remember, any of these fixes will help only for a very short time.

Lacing Boots

To provide adequate support, the boot must be properly laced. Proper lacing is necessary for keeping the foot secure in the boot and at the same time allowing the ankle freedom for movement. Nylon laces are recommended over cotton because they provide more flexibility.

Here are some quick hints for proper lacing:

- Lacing should be snug and firm from behind the ball of the foot up to the ankle. This provides support to the ankles and feet and helps to prevent injury.
- Press the heel firmly against the back of the boot while lacing.
- Make sure the tongue is pulled fully forward and is lying flat before you begin lacing.
- For a more secure fit, apply equal pressure to both ends of the ties while lacing.
- Lace tightly up to the hooks, then twist the laces twice below the ankle bend to prevent the laces from becoming loose.
- Continue lacing with moderate firmness to the top.

Ill-fitting boots can affect a skater's ability to perform spins and land jumps.

- When lacing is completed there should be a snug but not tight feeling.
- When the boot has been laced properly, you should be able to insert two fingers at the top and back of the boot.
- After tying a double bow knot securely at the top of the boot, tuck in the slack laces for safety and for a neat appearance.

Tips for Ensuring a Perfect Fit

In general, the more advanced the skater, the greater the requirement for support and stiffer boots. Keep the following helpful tips in mind when selecting and fitting boots:

• Too stiff a boot acts as a crutch. A firm boot is needed for support for double jumps, but just how firm depends on the skater. Some skaters are harder on boots than others and need stronger skates. Others are light on the ice and prefer a boot that provides support without restricting movement. Coaches can help assess a skater's needs.

• The number of hours a student skates per day influences the type of boot required. Boots are like tires on your car. The greater the mileage, the shorter the life. Boots that fit well and are properly cared for last longer than those that are not. A skater who is practicing double and triple jumps will wear boots out faster than a skater who is doing only single jumps or dance steps.

• A skater's physical build may determine the stiffness of boot required and may affect the skater's ability to break in the boot correctly. Remember that the tighter the boot is fitted when new, the less it will stretch when it is used.

• A thin child may have a sensitive foot from lack of cushioning. A bony foot requires more padding because of the sensitivity of the foot. You can easily request a boot with ample padding.

• A skater's test level and level of jumping and spinning ability influence the type of boot chosen. Some boots are extremely rigid—almost like a ski boot. This type of boot is needed for a heavier skater doing intermediate jumps or a lighter skater doing advanced jumps. Dance or team skaters may require specialized boots.

• The shape of a skater's foot may affect the choice of boot manufacturer. Most boots, even custom ones, are built on a model called a *last*. Some manufacturers use a wider or narrower last as their model. As with shoes, some brands may cater to more of a pointed toe and others to a more boxy look.

• If a skater needs a combination boot—a boot with a smaller heel than ball—look for a manufacturer that offers this feature. Some skaters do both freestyle and team skating. Others do dance and singles. In the beginning stages, a combination boot is all that is required. As skaters progress, however, they will want to purchase specialized boots for each discipline.

• Used boots can be a terrific choice if they fit properly and are not broken down. Too heavy or too strong a boot may be painful to break in and may result in foot damage or other problems later on. A beginning skater is able to use more advanced equipment if the stiff leather has been softened by a previous owner.

• Dance boots should be sturdy and give support, yet they must be flexible enough to allow for deep knee bends.

Boot Maintenance

According to major boot makers, the length of time that skating boots last depends on four factors:

1. Level of skater
2. Size and weight of skater

3. Type of boot being worn

4. Maintenance and care of boots

The well-known boot maker Riedell explains that material deterioration due to shoe aging is the number one reason that skating boots prematurely break down and wear out. Shoe aging occurs as a result of thermal or chemical forces emanating from the foot inside the shoe.

Perspiration is one example. Composed of 98 percent moisture and 2 percent salts and acids, it is a formidable element in shoe deterioration. About 60 percent of perspiration evaporates, but the remaining 40 percent is absorbed by the boot. The salts and acids become fixed inside the boot leather and have a significant corrosive effect.

Bacterial growth is another factor. The foot and shoe contain more active bacteria than any other part of the body. Bacteria eat protein, and leather is 98 percent protein.

The best way to extend the life of boots is to properly maintain them. To prolong the life of the boots, follow these steps:

- Waterproof the boots to prevent the soles from rotting.
- Wipe off interior and exterior moisture after every use.
- Let the boots dry between skating sessions.
- Use leather protectants when appropriate.
- Reseal with beeswax such as Sno-seal—every two months for skaters who are on the ice four to five days a week.

Choosing Blades

There are many blades on the market, and it is sometimes difficult to decide which one to recommend. There are two major blade manufacturers: John Wilson and Mitchel and King (MK). In general, the longer the blade, the more flow and glide you have on it. Shorter blades are better for maneuverability. A blade with more rock (a more curved profile) produces cleaner turns but may be more difficult to handle. A dance blade is thinner, has a shorter heel, and is flatter in profile than a freestyle blade.

There are four elements to consider when choosing a blade:

1. **Radius of hollow**—The radius of hollow refers to the curved groove that runs along the bottom of the blade. The deeper the hollow, the more the blade grips the ice. (This is explained further in the section on blade sharpening.)

2. **Rocker radius**—The profile of a blade is curved rather than straight, as you might think. The rocker of the blade is defined by how much the blade curves from toe to heel. Because of this curve, placing blades end to end forms a circle that, when measured, determines the rocker radius.

3. **Blade type**—There are four types of blades: parallel, tapered, dovetail, and slimline. (See figure 2.1.) The most common is the parallel blade, which has the same width from toe to heel. A tapered blade is wider at the front of the blade and is thinned consistently down the length of the blade to the tail. Tapered blades are also side hollow ground, which is the removal of the steel at the factory to reduce blade weight to provide more defined edges and

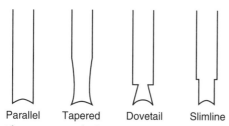

Parallel   Tapered   Dovetail   Slimline

Figure 2.1 Blade types.

increased angle to the ice for tighter turns. The dovetail blade also provides more defined edges and increased angle to the ice, but is a parallel-type blade. Slimline blades have a thinner blade for quicker changes from edge to edge.

4. **Size**—Blades come in sizes listed in one-quarter inch increments.

Prices vary depending on the manufacturer, the quality of the steel, and the use or type of skating that the blade is intended for. Table 2.1 will help you understand the types of blades that are available. The most expensive blade is listed at the top of each category.

In selecting blades, you have to consider the individual skater. The beginning or preliminary skater does fine with a good all-around blade that can be used for all types of figure skating. The advanced freestyle skater may need a blade with larger toe picks to assist in the takeoff of jumps.

Although blade sizes do not vary, boots do vary in their outer sole length. Therefore, two boots of the same size may have different sole measurements and use different size blades. Once a boot has been chosen, measure its length from toe to heel and fit blades that are one-quarter inch less in length. If a one-quarter inch difference is not possible, always err on the long side for the blade.

After you've found the right blades, ask an experienced staff member to mount them to the boots. Be aware of the following to ensure that the blades are mounted correctly:

Table 2.1 Blade Models and Dimensions

	John Wilson — For the recreational skater to the serious competitor					**Mitchel & King** — For the recreational skater to the serious competitor				
Usage	Model	Radius of hollow	Rocker radius	Blade type	Sizes	Model	Radius of hollow	Rocker radius	Blade type	Sizes
Freestyle	Gold Seal	1/2 in.	8 ft.	Tapered	8–12	Gold Star Chrome	7/8 in.	7 ft.	Tapered	8–12
	Pattern 99	5/8 in.	8 ft.	Parallel	8–12	Phantom Special	7/8 in.	7 ft.	Dovetail	8–12
	Coronation Comet	5/8 in.	8.5 ft.	Parallel	7.5–12	Phantom	7/8 in.	7 ft.	Tapered	7–12
	Coronation Ace	5/8 in.	7 ft.	Parallel	6–12.25	Vision	7/8 in.	7 ft.	Parallel	7.5–12
						Professional	7/8 in.	7 ft.	Parallel	8–12
Dance, team	Super Dance 99	5/8 in.	8 ft.	Parallel	8–12	Dance	5/8 in.	7 ft.	Parallel	8–12
	Precision	5/8 in.	8 ft.	Parallel	8–12	Precision	7/8 in.	7 ft.	Parallel	8–12
	Coronation Dance	5/8 in.	7 ft.	Parallel	8–12					
General purpose	Majestic	5/8 in.	7 ft.	Parallel	5.75–12.25	Double Star	1 in.	7 ft.	Parallel	6–12.25
	PSA	3/4 in.	7 ft.	Parallel	6–12					

Blades come in the sizes listed above in 1/4 inch increments.

- The center of the sole and the center of the heel of the boot must be in exact alignment. Otherwise, stress is placed on the blade during mounting and the blade becomes bent.
- The front of the long axis of the blade should be between the big and second toe.
- The rear stanchion should be at the center or slightly to the inside of the heel.
- Flat-headed screws should be used in the slotted holes and tapered screws used in the recessed holes.

Blade Maintenance

Blade maintenance includes the following:

- Blades must be dried carefully after each use.
- Guards should be placed on the blades at all times when skates are worn off ice to protect blades from nicks and from the damaging effect of salt, sand, and other corrosives.
- Guards should be removed when storing blades to prevent water damage.
- Blades should generally be sharpened after every 20 to 25 sessions on the ice.
- Blades should be sharpened correctly.

Blade Sharpening

Running the entire length of the bottom of a blade is a curved groove known as the hollow. The degree of the curvature of this hollow is expressed by the radius of the circle of which the hollow is a part. The blade is relatively thin, so this curvature is hard to estimate. You can get a rough idea of the depth of hollow by placing coins in the groove, but accurate gauges do exist and the best sharpeners possess them.

The greater the depth of the hollow, the more the blade will sink into the ice. The flatter the hollow, the less the blade penetrates the ice surface. A deeper hollow produces a greater grip, but this is not always an advantage. For example, the takeoff to a double Axel almost invariably involves a skid at the end of the takeoff edge, and the depth of the hollow greatly influences the length of skid that can be comfortably made. For this reason, skaters who are used to a certain depth of hollow often lose control of the takeoff edge just after their blades have been sharpened to a slightly deeper hollow.

Every skater gets used to a certain depth of hollow that suits his or her techniques. As a rough guide, many elite skaters use a three-eighths inch radius (or sometimes even deeper), whereas others may prefer the slightly flatter hollow of a five-eighths inch radius. Ice dancers who use a thinner blade usually require a deeper hollow to achieve the same angle of cutting edge. For skaters who skate figures, a much flatter sharpening is usually required because it tends to make possible more accuracy in the turns.

The section on blade sharpening was written by Robert Ogilvie and edited by Carole Shulman. Ogilvie is the designer and author of the USFSA Basic Test program and the author of many books on skating, including *Basic Ice Skating Skills* and *Competitive Figure Skating—A Parent's Guide*. He hails from Great Britain and was a competitor in World and European Pair Championships and a reserve member of the British Olympic Pair team. He holds master ratings in figures, freestyle, pairs, and group skating, as well as in program administration.

Keep in mind the following guidelines for sharpening blades:

- Sharpening a blade consists primarily of restoring the existing hollow.
- As soon as you are comfortable with a certain degree of hollow, ask your sharpener what the radius of the hollow is and mark it on the inside of the boot so that you will not forget it.
- Do not allow your blades to get so dull that even if the correct hollow is restored you may at first think they are too sharp.
- Do not assume that the hollow of a new blade as put in at the factory necessarily suits your requirements.
- Know your sharpener.
- If you change sharpeners and your blades seem very dull, do not assume your blades have been ruined. It's more likely that you have been unable to tell the sharpener exactly what hollow you require.
- The decision about what hollow you require is your responsibility, not the sharpener's. Not knowing what hollow you use is similar to an elite tennis player's not knowing the tension of his racket.
- Check your blades before a competition. Do not go to your pro the night before and say you think you need your skates sharpened.

A good sharpener should do the following:

- Sharpen the blade without altering the profile of the blade or the rocker radius
- Keep the edges of the blade level
- Not interfere with the toe rakes unless instructed to do so
- Not overheat the blade while sharpening
- Preserve a reasonably smooth finish to the blade
- Be able to put a specific hollow into the blade or maintain the current one
- Advise the customer without dictating
- Have a good knowledge of the customer's branch of the sport

To repeat one highly important piece of advice, learn and remember the specific depth of hollow that suits you.

Dressed for Success

Practice wear should be comfortable, allow for freedom of movement, and be attractive. Most skaters dress in layers so that they can remove their sweaters or jackets once they are warmed up, then put these items on again during the cool-down. It is always a good idea to practice with gloves or mittens.

Girls wear tights to protect their legs from ice burns and scrapes when the inevitable falls occur. Women usually wear leotards, dresses, or skirts and tops. Men wear leotards or pants and shirts. Clothing made from Lycra is very popular for both men and women because of its stretching quality. It also breathes, allowing for some warmth while not trapping body moisture in when the workouts become more heated. Matching sweaters or lightweight jackets add a complementary touch to the outfit and serve a useful function in warming the body.

Competition outfits are similar to practice outfits but dressier. In the same way you would compare eveningwear to daytime clothing, competition wear is designed to be flattering to the body and reflective of the theme or mood of the music. It usually is enhanced with rhinestones or sequins. Jewels can be added to men's costumes as well as women's. Skaters together with their coaches are responsible for deciding on the appropriate wear for competition.

Summary

The coach and skater alike should be informed about skating equipment and know the skater's personal parameters. Key items to consider when selecting boots are how hard the skater is on boots, the level of skating ability, the level of discipline, and any particular foot shape or problems such as a high arch or a narrow heel.

Because of the outstanding selection of fabrics today, clothing for skating can meet everyone's needs. When well constructed, these fabrics can fit comfortably, move freely, and look attractive. By wearing a sweater or lightweight jacket, the skater can add warmth when necessary at the beginning of the session and remove layers as the practice progresses.

Once the skater is fitted correctly and dressed appropriately, the lessons can begin. Because off-ice conditioning is also important, the next chapter addresses physical fitness.

© Bob Tringali/SportsChrome USA

Competition outfits, like the one worn here by Maria Butyrskaya, are designed to complement the skater's body and reflect the theme of the music.

chapter 3
Skating Fitness

Years ago people thought that anyone who wanted to become a better skater should simply spend more hours on the ice. Today's coaches know that what skaters do off the ice can speed up their progress as well. Strength training, flexibility exercises, cross-training, and plyometric drills are a few ways to learn skills more quickly and improve their level of performance. For example, a skater who is ready to begin learning a double Axel can choose to learn either by the fall-and-get-up method on the ice, or to shorten the learning curve by building upper-body strength using free weights. Under proper supervision this second method reduces the chance of injury, builds the strength needed to increase rotation, and decreases the amount of time it takes to master the jump.

Skaters can also improve their performance and speed recovery through proper nutrition. It's important to give the body the fuel it needs for both on- and off-ice training. To do otherwise not only adversely affects performance but also increases the risk of injury.

Off-Ice Conditioning

At the 2000 U.S. National Championships, Timothy Goebel successfully landed three quadruple jumps. This unbelievable accomplishment illustrates the future of skating and the technical prowess that skaters must achieve to become national, world, and Olympic contenders. To land a quadruple 10 years ago was unthinkable. Back then skaters were struggling to land triples. Today, off-ice conditioning has made the impossible possible.

Higher physical demands have been placed not only on the singles skater; dance teams and pair skaters must also participate in power-building activities such as weight training. Even synchronized skating teams are beginning to incorporate an off-ice training program into their scheduled activities.

Strength Training

Strength is the ability of the muscles to produce internal tension and exert resistance against external forces. Strength is an essential component in skating performance, overall physical fitness, and the functioning of the cardiac, respiratory, and metabolic systems.

Skaters can improve their performance by doing exercises that build strength to resist gravitational forces in jumping or spinning. For example, pair skaters build strength so that in a lift each partner is able to press against the other and sustain the force necessary to hold the lift.

The first step in designing a strength training program is to define all the major categories of strength so that you can determine which type of strength you want your program to emphasize. A skater who tends to tire excessively during a program, making an unusually high number of mistakes toward the program's end, should take part in a strength training program that emphasizes muscular endurance. A male pair skater who does not have the strength to support his partner in an overhead lift should concentrate on a program that increases maximal strength levels.

Before you start, keep in mind that some off-ice activities, like strength training, do present a potential for injury to the athlete, so it is important for a qualified trainer

---

This chapter was written with help from Kim Goss, who has been designing off-ice conditioning programs for figure skaters since 1988. Coach Goss currently lives in Dallas, Texas, where he trains skaters full time.

Strength training can help build the strength and endurance needed to perform challenging moves, like this lift by Xue Shen and Hongbo Zhao.

to supervise the program you set up. The strength coach can set up a long-term planning approach to training, called periodization, which ensures that the skater is at a physical peak for competition. It is not enough that the trainer be qualified for strength training. The trainer must also understand skating; appreciate the differing needs of the singles, pair, dance, or team skater; and be willing to work with skating coaches.

Classifications of Strength

There are several classifications of strength quality, but the types most relevant to skaters are maximal strength, absolute strength, relative strength, optimal strength, strength endurance, and speed strength.

- **Maximal strength** is the most force the muscles can voluntarily produce in a single contraction, irrespective of the time element. Maximal strength can be broken down into three types of muscular contractions:
  1. Concentric contraction—If a muscle develops tension, shortens, and produces movement, that activity is referred to as a concentric contraction. A powerful concentric contraction of the quadriceps, hamstrings, and gluteal muscles enables a freestyle skater to jump high into the air and a dancer to stroke harder and faster.
  2. Isometric contraction—If a muscle develops tension but does not produce movement of the body part it is attached to, that activity is referred to as an isometric contraction. An isometric contraction of the hamstring muscles helps a skater to hold a high spiral or a male pair skater to support his partner in an overhead lift.
  3. Eccentric contraction—If a muscle lengthens while producing tension, thus braking or controlling the speed of the movement, that activity is referred to as an eccentric contraction. An eccentric contraction supports a skater on the landing of a jump.

- **Absolute strength** is the maximum force an athlete can produce, regardless of body weight and time of force development. Absolute strength is most relevant to male pair skaters as they must support their partners in overhead lifts.

- **Relative strength** is the maximum force an athlete can generate per unit of body weight, irrespective of time of force development. This is important to skaters as they want to be as strong as possible without carrying a large amount of muscle bulk.

- **Optimal strength** is the ideal level of strength a skater needs so that any further development would not enhance performance. There is a limit to the amount of strength training a figure skater needs, in contrast to a sport such as powerlifting in which the more strength you possess, the more successful you become. In skating, increasing strength should not detract from other important aspects of training such as ballet or jazz or on-ice stroking.

- **Strength endurance** refers to an athlete's tolerance to muscle fatigue. Because jumping and stroking make significant demands on the muscular system, high levels of strength endurance enable skaters to perform their best throughout the entire program.

- **Speed strength** is the ability to produce the greatest possible force in the shortest possible time frame. There are three types of speed strength:
  1. Starting strength—Starting strength is the ability to produce a high level of force at the beginning of a muscular contraction. It is the capacity to overcome resistance and initiate movement, such as when jumping.
  2. Explosive strength—Explosive strength is the capacity to develop a sharp, sudden rise in force once movement has been initiated, such as when stroking.

3. Reactive strength—Reactive strength is the ability to quickly switch from an eccentric contraction to a concentric contraction, such as when executing combination jumps. The start of a jump begins with a knee bend, and then the leg straightens as it presses against the ice for the liftoff. Because the body has the capacity to use stored energy, high levels of reactive strength enable a skater to jump higher by shortening the pause between the eccentric and concentric contractions of the leg muscles.

Strength Training Variables

Just as skating is a complex activity, there are also many factors involved in designing a strength training program. Once a skater and coach have determined which type of strength to focus on, the next step is to look at each of the variables involved in designing a strength training program, including the amount of resistance, the number of reps and sets to perform, and how much rest time to take between sets.

Amount of resistance.   The amount of resistance used in an exercise is one of the most important variables that determine the training effect. This is because the heavier the weight used, the more tension is imposed on a muscle, and this tension determines the training response. But instead of using the term *tension* to describe the training effect of a workout, strength coaches prefer the term *intensity.*

Reps.   Because a beginner's nervous system is not as developed as an advanced athlete's, beginners tend to respond better to higher repetitions. Thus, a beginner might develop higher strength levels by performing sets of 10 reps rather than 5 reps.

Sets.   After repetitions are determined, the number of sets must also be decided. There is an inverse relationship between sets and reps: The fewer reps performed, the more sets needed to achieve the appropriate training response.

As athletes become stronger, they must perform more total reps to achieve the desired training effect. This type of adaptation response is one reason elite weightlifters must often work out several times a day, five to six days a week—it is the only way they can continue making progress.

Tempo.   Another factor that affects the training response is lifting speed, or tempo. Lifting at slow speeds is associated with the fastest increases in muscle mass. Lifting slowly eliminates the use of momentum to lift the resistance, which in turn increases tension on the muscle. In contrast, lifting weights faster may increase an athlete's ability to display force more rapidly.

The tempo enables athletes to enjoy greater control over the training effect. For example, a skater who has trouble holding landings could perform leg exercises with longer eccentric phases. When using tempo prescriptions, it's important to recognize that the total amount of time it takes to perform an exercise influences the training response.

As a general guideline, for increases in maximal strength a set should take less than 20 seconds to perform; for maximal increases in muscle mass approximately 60 seconds of tension are most effective; and for increases in strength endurance more than 60 seconds should be used. Remember that these are only general guidelines, as many factors influence the training response, such as the amount of weight training experience the athlete possesses.

Rest.　The amount of rest taken between sets also influences the training effect. For developing maximal or relative strength, rest intervals of three to five minutes are appropriate; for hypertrophy, two to three minutes; and for strength endurance, less than two minutes.

Duration.　This is the amount of time taken from the start of a workout to the finish, not including warm-up or cool-down. It is a combination of the number of exercises, reps, and sets performed; the tempo used; and the length of the rest periods.

The modern trend in weight training is to keep workouts short. Workouts exceeding one hour have been associated with rapidly decreasing androgen levels. These rapid decreases are believed to have an adverse effect on the testosterone/cortisol ratio, which is strongly related to strength gains. For advanced athletes who must achieve high strength gains, multiple workouts are recommended with at least a one-hour break between workouts to allow testosterone levels to return to normal.

Frequency.　This refers to the number of training sessions per week. Many factors affect frequency. To achieve higher levels of conditioning, more frequent workouts are required. Whereas a beginner can make progress on two workouts a week, a higher-level athlete might require ten times that many to continue making progress. However, if a skater is under considerable stress, working especially hard, or spending more time on the ice, the number of weight training workouts must be reduced to avoid overtraining.

Exercise Selection

One of the most important decisions strength coaches must make in designing off-ice conditioning programs is selecting the exercises their athletes perform. It is also one of their most difficult responsibilities, as there are literally thousands of exercises for each body part.

Unfortunately, there is no simple answer to the question of what exercises are best for skaters, because there are many variables to consider. One of the best ways to select the appropriate exercises for workouts is the method popularized by Canadian strength coach Charles Poliquin, which uses a process of elimination by asking the following six questions:

1. *What are the training goals?* Are the primary goals of off-ice conditioning to improve a skater's jumping ability, prevent injuries, or create a more aesthetic appearance on the ice? After determining the primary goals of the off-ice conditioning program, the strength coach can set about designing a plan to achieve those goals.

2. *What muscles are most important to achieving the training goals?* Often strength coaches find that by identifying the muscles important to achieving the training goals, they can design more efficient workouts to achieve those goals. An excessively forward head posture may be caused primarily by a weakness in the abdominal muscles known as the external obliques, instead of the neck muscles that retract the head.

3. *Which muscles are assistors?* Although it is convenient to say that one muscle is the cause and one exercise is the solution, the reality is usually not that simple. Other muscles are often involved.

4. *Which muscles are antagonistic?* Workouts that emphasize only specific muscle groups often produce muscle imbalances. If skaters work the muscles of the chest that help pull in the arms, for example, but neglect the opposing (antagonistic) back muscles, they sometimes create muscle imbalances that adversely affect the posture of the spine.

5. *Which muscles are stabilizers?* When the muscles that stabilize a joint are underdeveloped, muscle weakness occurs and joint stability is compromised. One reason skaters should avoid exercises with machines is that they don't work these stabilizer muscles.

6. *Which muscles should be stressed at which times during the training year?* Finally, it's important to know when in the training year to emphasize certain exercises, especially exercise methods such as plyometrics that can be very stressful on the joints and tissue. For example, practicing plyometric exercises before a major competition, when skaters are performing numerous jumps on the ice, may push athletes into overtraining and leave them unable to give their best performance.

These questions require considerable thought to answer, but answering them as precisely as possible is necessary to ensure that the athlete receives the best training possible.

Exercise Order

The method by which the exercises are arranged in a workout also affects the training response. For example, athletes who want to improve upper-body strength enjoy greater strength training response if they perform upper-body exercise early in their programs. As a general guideline, exercises that are complex, work large muscle groups, or are designed to improve speed strength should be performed early in the workout. However, the strength coach should depart from these guidelines if they conflict with the training goal.

One popular system of arranging the order of exercises is called circuit training. According to exercise scientist Mel Siff, PhD, in his book *Supertraining,* R. Morgan and G. Adamson introduced circuit training in 1953 at the University of Leeds in England as a way to simultaneously integrate several components of fitness. In contrast to conventional training (also called *station training*), which entails performing all sets of an exercise before moving to another, circuit training consists of performing one set of each exercise in a series, or *circuit,* of exercises. One circuit might consist of 10 reps of bench presses, 10 reps of leg presses, and 10 reps of chin-ups.

In the 1970s circuit training got a boost when Arthur Jones introduced his single-station Nautilus machines, aesthetically appealing stations that were ideally suited for this form of training. Circuit training is still used today, but because this type of training monopolizes numerous pieces of equipment at once it is not considered practical in many training environments.

Although there are many types of circuit training, the two basic types commonly used are *anaerobic* (non-oxidative) and *aerobic* (oxidative) circuits. Variety is essential to any conditioning program to ensure continual progress and to prevent mental staleness. Ways to instill variety in circuit training include changing the exercises performed, the number of exercise stations, the number of reps and circuits performed, the tempo of each exercise, and the length of the rest intervals.

Periodization

Periodization is the process of manipulating all the major variables of training so that athletes perform their best at their most important competitions. For an elite skater, this may mean reaching a peak for the world championships, whereas for a beginner this may mean peaking for a regional championship.

In skating, you may divide the training year into periods by first concentrating on new jumps, then choreographing a new program, then finally putting the jumps into the program. You shouldn't try to work on all these aspects of skating at once, because they all take a considerable amount of time to achieve, and there is only so much time available for most athletes to devote to training. Furthermore, each cycle builds on the results achieved in the previous cycles. For example, if a new jump is mastered during the first phase of training, this could affect how the program is choreographed in the next phase of training.

When you apply periodization to a strength training program, you manipulate all the variables of strength training introduced earlier according to your training goals. For example, a skater may want to concentrate on increasing relative strength early in the season, then change the focus to strength endurance after the competitive season.

The sample 18-week weight training program that follows begins by focusing on muscle mass, then absolute strength, then relative strength. It uses a linear design, progressing from high reps to low reps. This program is merely an example; a specific program should be designed for each skater, taking into account the athlete's age, size, ability, level, and progress. The program will also vary based on whether the athlete is a singles, pair, or dance skater.

Weeks	Reps
1–3	12
4–6	10
7–9	8
10–12	6
13–15	4
16–18	3

An alternative approach that uses an undulating design looks like this:

Weeks	Reps
1–3	12
4–6	6
7–9	10
10–12	4
13–15	8
16–18	3

This second approach is considered more effective because it provides greater variations between each training phase, and as athletes reach higher levels of conditioning they respond better to programs that have a greater variety of stimuli between training phases. Also, because a higher number of reps is performed in the later phases, the gains in muscle mass do not diminish as much as with the linear approach to training.

Flexibility Training

No discussion of off-ice conditioning would be complete without mentioning stretching. Stretching goes beyond injury prevention and rehabilitation. Exceptional levels of flexibility are required for spirals, split jumps, Biellmann spins, and pair and dance moves. Stretching can also improve posture, which, in turn, improves performance and enhances presentation. Flexibility takes years to develop and daily workouts to maintain, so it is important to follow proper guidelines from the beginning.

Flexibility is a necessity when it comes to performing moves like this spin by Irina Slutskaya.

One basic way to improve flexibility is through static stretching. With this type of stretching, muscles are passively lengthened and then held in the stretched position for prolonged periods of time. In contrast, in dynamic stretching the muscles are taken to extreme ranges of motion rapidly but under muscular control, such as with ballet training or the martial arts. Here are some dos and don'ts of static stretching:

- Do stretch in the proper environment. A firm nonskid mat is ideal. The area the athlete stretches in should be free from distractions. The area should not be at the dasher boards on the ice or in a cold area of the rink.
- Do warm up before stretching. The goal of the warm-up is to raise the body temperature so that the muscles can be stretched more effectively. You can accomplish this objective with a few minutes of low-intensity activities such as jogging or light calisthenics. It is also a good idea to move each joint through its full range of motion (and even shake it out) before stretching.
- Do stretch the muscles one joint at a time. Muscles work in pairs, so it is best to design a stretching program that addresses these opposing pairs. For example, after athletes stretch the quadriceps they should stretch the hamstrings.
- Do stretch the tightest muscles first. A tight muscle can inhibit the stretch of collaborating muscles.
- Do take it slow. Athletes should move gradually into each stretch and ease out of every stretch smoothly.
- Do concentrate on breathing. Proper breathing methods can significantly enhance the quality of a stretching program. Athletes should begin each stretch by holding their breath, then gently exhaling and easing deeper into the stretch. At the next breath they should ease up on the stretch a bit, inhale and hold the breath again, then gently exhale and try to stretch even farther.
- Do listen to pain. The athlete shouldn't force a joint to the point of feeling pain or discomfort.
- Do vary the orientation of the stretches and the types of stretches. For example, when a hamstring stretch is performed with a straight leg in front, the stretch could later be varied by rotating the foot. Each small adjustment in a stretch, even varying the arm position, can hit different regions of the muscle to ensure optimal levels of flexibility for the muscles.
- Do personalize your stretching. A stretch coach must consider individual needs when designing a stretching program. A male pair skater, for example, may not need as much flexibility training as his partner.
- Do stretch after skating. Stretching after a skating session is especially effective because the muscles are warm and because stretching at this time can help prevent excessive muscle tension (much more so than if the athlete waits several hours before stretching).
- Do pay attention to the duration of the stretch. An athlete enjoys the most benefit by holding each position for at least 30 seconds. Less than this may not produce the results expected, and more than this may simply be a waste of time.
- Don't stretch immediately before skating. Doing so can interfere with a skater's ability to contract the muscles maximally for jumping.

- Don't stretch the muscles around an area that has been recently injured, sprained, strained, or fractured, especially around the back or neck. Stretching these muscles could aggravate the condition.

Plyometrics

One aspect of off-ice conditioning that has attracted considerable interest in the skating community is a training method called plyometrics, which are special jump exercises that make use of the body's ability to store and release energy. These exercises can improve many aspects of athletic conditioning, especially jumping ability, without developing a significant degree of muscle mass. Many skaters, particularly elite skaters, use this type of training to reach the highest levels of athletic ability.

Because of the stress these exercises can place on the body, you must be careful about including plyometric training exercises into an off-ice conditioning program. This is especially true with athletes who have a history of injuries to the lower extremities. Also, a naturally gifted jumper may not benefit as much from a plyometric program as a less-gifted jumper and may be better off concentrating on other aspects of off-ice conditioning.

Cross-Training

The practice of using another sport to supplement a primary sport is called cross-training. This approach can be great for developing an off-ice training program. Improved performance and reduced risk of injury are among the benefits. Cross-training can also help correct muscle imbalances and generate enthusiasm and participation in off-ice training.

Obvious cross-training sports for figure skaters are gymnastics, in-line skating, and jogging. But also consider rock climbing for upper-body strength, cycling for quad strength and endurance, the martial arts for flexibility, and tennis for abdominal strength. These activities also develop coordination, balance, and muscular endurance, in addition to providing recreational pleasure.

At the same time, be aware of adverse effects that can result from cross-training. For example, because the jumping techniques in gymnastics are different from those in skating, gymnastics may not be a good cross-training activity for a high-level skater. Moreover, the stress that gymnastics places on the lower extremities may significantly increase the risk of a skater becoming injured. As such, all cross-training activities must be considered with good sense, be done in moderation, and prove to be particularly beneficial if continued on a routine basis.

The psychological benefits of cross-training are also worth considering. Simply performing any other sport can provide a mental vacation, reduce stress, and be a way to discover new, fun ways to enjoy oneself. Lyn St. James of the Women's Sport Foundation (WSF) and racecar fame had a theory that most good athletes have abilities that would transfer from one sport to another, giving that athlete an advantage over someone who had not previously participated in another sport. St. James proved her theory when she invited Billie Jean King to join her on the racetrack. The eye-hand coordination that King had developed on the tennis court placed her in good stead behind the wheel of a race car. Another carryover was her ability to think quickly in her seat as well as on her feet. After the initial experiment, several women in the WSF traded sports and had an enjoyable time trying something new and discovering they were good at it!

Cross-training can be performed on the same day as the athlete's primary sport (usually after the primary sport), on a day off, or in the off season. The concept that you can "play yourself into shape," however, is simply not true. A regimented off-ice training program is required, and cross-training is one way to help skaters develop the athletic fitness they need to achieve their goals.

Home Training

Because of many skaters' busy schedules, it is often not practical for them to train at a gym, and few ice rinks have on-site weight training facilities. An alternative is home training. When skaters work out at home they enjoy the convenience of being able to train whenever they please, without having to wait for equipment. They also save time by not having to travel back and forth to the gym, and they can save money in the long run by not having to pay gym fees.

If a skater decides to train at home, the first thing to do is to establish a specific place to work out. One excellent place for home training is a guest room. By clearing out some furniture and substituting a rollaway or small daybed in place of a larger bed, a guest room can be transformed into a home gym within a few minutes. There are many possibilities, and it takes some serious planning to decide which place is best.

To increase the chance of success with a home training program, here are a few pointers:

• *Make a workout appointment.* If skaters expect to get serious results from training at home, they have to train seriously, and this means scheduling specific times for their workouts. Skaters should schedule appointments for their workouts and treat them as seriously as they would a dentist appointment.

Often the best time to work out is the first thing in the morning. Besides reducing the risk of missing a workout in the evening because "something came up" (something as trivial as MTV or as legitimate as homework), training in the morning increases circulation, giving athletes a cardiovascular jump-start for the day. And because they have accomplished something that has a positive impact on their health, they start the day with a positive attitude.

• *Work out in gym clothes.* Going through the ritual of putting on workout clothes helps get athletes in the proper mindset to work out. After all, if they take the time to change into workout attire but only exercise for ten minutes or less, it's barely worth the effort. Also, exercising in street clothes could restrict the range of motion in many exercises (especially lunges and squats), thereby reducing the effectiveness of the workout. What's more, if the workout area is too cold or too hot and athletes are not dressed appropriately, the risk of injury increases.

• *Train alone or with a serious training partner.* Unless additional people are there to provide a spot for high-risk weight training exercises, it's usually not a good idea to allow family or friends to watch a skater work out. Conversations with friends and family can ruin concentration and training pace, and they can even increase the risk of injury by distracting the athlete. Skaters need to be able to focus on their training, especially if they are lifting weights. They should let everybody know that this is their time and that they are not to be disturbed.

On the other hand, it's often a good idea to find someone to work out with (and, of course, very young skaters should *always* have adult supervision). A serious training partner helps create a good workout environment, as the partners can encourage each other to train harder.

- *Play music and exercise videos.* Playing upbeat music enhances the workout atmosphere. Many health clubs, especially the hardcore ones, play lots of hard rock, which can often be more irritating than inspiring. At home skaters can enjoy the music that creates a stimulating workout environment for them.

- *Chart progress.* By simply checking off on a calendar when they train or by filling out all the details of their workouts in a professional training log, skaters who chart their progress receive valuable feedback about their training and keep themselves motivated.

- *Provide rewards.* One way to keep motivation high is for skaters to give themselves small rewards when they accomplish significant goals during their workouts. Off-ice training can be fun, but it can also be hard work, so skaters shouldn't hesitate to give themselves a reward for a job well done!

Nutrition

One of the most common questions asked about nutrition is this: How do skaters meet their nutritional requirements when they're in training? They have hectic schedules with on-ice and off-ice practices, and they juggle skating with school or work. It seems there is little time to stop and eat a balanced meal.

The answer is simple, but the discipline in carrying out the solution is not so easy until a routine is established. First a skater must drink plenty of fluids and eat low-fat, high-carbohydrate foods on a daily basis—and daily does mean every day! For optimal performance, an athlete's diet should consist of 60 to 65 percent carbohydrate calories, 12 to 15 percent protein calories, and 25 to 30 percent fat calories. It is especially important for a skater to store up carbs the day before a competition and immediately after a workout or practice session.

Skaters should eat or drink 200 to 400 carbohydrate calories right after exercise and again two hours later. A quick and easy way to do this is to drink eight ounces of a fruit juice or a sport drink such as Gatorade or AllSport. These items can easily be placed in a skate bag so that they are available after a workout. Many rinks have machines that dispense juice or they are often available at the concession stand.

Fruits and vegetables are other quick and easy sources of carbohydrates. Apples, bananas, oranges, dates, and apricots are fruits that are easy to place in a skate bag or backpack. They are especially handy if they are already peeled or prepared for eating and placed in a plastic bag. Sliced carrots are also an easy and quick snack food that skaters can carry with them or eat in the car as they are traveling to and from home, school, gym, or rink.

Other good, portable sources of carbohydrates are bagels, English muffins, crackers, pretzels, popcorn, and sport bars. Less easy to carry but good for skaters are cereals (especially unsweetened), pancakes, tortillas, pasta, steamed vegetables, baked potatoes, and milk.

For optimal performance, it is also important for skaters to include iron in their diets. Finger foods such as peanuts, raisins, or sunflower seeds are good sources of iron. Prepared the night before and taken on the go, a lean ham or turkey sandwich is a great source of iron. Juices rich in iron are tomato and prune juice, which are easily found in cans in the grocery store. For breakfast or between meals, try instant breakfast drinks. Skaters should try to include three iron-rich foods in their diet each day.

What about protein? Most people eat more protein than they need. Skaters should concentrate on the carbs and iron and minimize the protein. However, lean sources of protein—such as chicken and other poultry, fish, and beans—are recommended for skaters.

By purchasing the right foods at the grocery store and planning ahead for busy days, skaters will be more apt to eat healthful foods and avoid snacking on fat-rich foods such as chips and french fries. A sound training program and good nutrition combine to make a winning performance.

Body Image and Dieting

At a training camp for figure skaters, a respected nutritionist gave a group of upcoming athletes a great seminar on sports nutrition. When the expert left the room, an influential judge told the skaters that the information they had just heard was sound but that "skating is an aesthetic sport, and you have to do what it takes to win." It is this typical attitude, based on ignorance, that has pushed many skaters into lifelong struggles with weight.

Concern, and sometimes even obsession, with body weight is something that affects both male and female athletes. This is especially true of athletes in sports that impose weight restrictions, as in figure skating and gymnastics. An undesired side effect of such restrictions is a deleterious means of weight loss. This trend is particularly prevalent in young to middle-aged females. As such, learning a few things about how females store and burn fat can go a long way toward preventing and resolving weight problems in skaters.

Females have more fat-storage enzymes than males. Fat regulates the production of estrogen, a hormone necessary for females to conceive and give birth. Unfortunately, having high estrogen levels also makes it easier for females to gain weight.

In *Outsmarting the Female Fat Cell*, Debra Waterhouse, MPH, RD, says that low-calorie diets can increase the number of fat-storing enzymes. Waterhouse says research conducted at Cedars-Sinai Medical Center found that diets that are too low in calories can actually double the number of these enzymes. Once a skater abandons such a diet and begins eating regularly, her body quickly regains the weight she lost—and more! This condition is commonly referred to as the yo-yo syndrome.

Just the fact that females diet more than males is a problem. When a female loses weight on a very low-calorie diet, her system may go into a *negative nitrogen balance*, a condition that causes the body to break down muscle tissue for fuel. Losing just a pound of muscle through this process can represent as much as a 50-calorie reduction in her daily caloric requirement.

How do skaters determine whether they are eating enough? When the body has a very low-calorie diet, the thyroid gland produces less of a chemical called triiodothyronine. Triiodothyronine helps regulate body temperature, one of the factors that determine metabolism (the rate at which a person burns calories). The most accurate way to determine thyroid function is a blood test, but a more practical method is by simply checking morning body temperature. A waking temperature below 98.2 degrees may be an indication that the thyroid is not functioning as it should and metabolism is slowing down. (An extremely low morning body temperature may also indicate other health problems, so a visit to a doctor would be wise.)

A skater who has been using a very low-calorie diet to lose weight needs to gradually work back to regular eating to avoid the rebound weight gain. Depending on how severe the diet was and how long the skater was on it, up to three months of careful diet management may be necessary to resume normal eating habits and to return thyroid levels to normal.

Although gradually increasing calories is one way to ensure that a rapid fat gain doesn't occur with a skater who isn't eating enough, a better approach is to use a rotation diet that varies caloric intake daily. For example, if a skater who needs 1,800 calories a day has been on a diet of 700 calories a day, she could work back to a regular diet faster by alternating diets of 900, 1,200, and 1,500 calories for several weeks before going back to a regular diet of 1,800 calories a day.

Unfortunately, there is no single diet that works for every person. Consulting with a nutritionist is the best first step toward designing the right nutrition program. But skaters must be patient. Finding that perfect diet is often a trial-and-error process that can seem to be as much an art as it is a science.

In most cases a good diet is common sense. When people work out, they require more fuel for the engine and they also need more muscle, which adds pounds and may cause concern to skaters whose body weight is higher than they think it should be. Because it is easy to lose perspective, it is a good idea to have a trusted coach or trainer advise skaters about diet and weight control.

The information on body image and dieting was taken from the *PSA Study Guide for the Basic Accreditation Exam* prepared by Janice M. Bibik, PhD, University of Delaware.

Summary

A complete skater must perform well, feel well inside and out, and look great, even while performing the most difficult program. Strength training, flexibility, and conditioning exercises are necessary in order to accomplish all this. In addition, skaters must provide their bodies with proper nutrition. It's the total package that allows athletes to skate their best. Once skaters understand their bodies and their nutritional needs, they are ready to commence training and enjoy skating to the best of their abilities.

part II
Techniques

chapter 4

The Basics: From Stops to Crossovers

© Claus Andersen

Skaters who perform the gravity-defying jumps and mind-boggling spins that dazzle audiences all over the world have one thing in common. They all draw on a set of fundamental techniques to do what they do. They glide powerfully across the ice, changing from edge to edge, leaping into the air, and stopping on a dime without giving these actions much thought. Mastering basic skating techniques is what enabled them to progress to such a high level.

This chapter describes how to perform fundamental skating techniques, including stops, forward and backward glides, sculling, outside and inside edges, and forward and backward crossovers. Skaters who become proficient at these basics will be on their way to learning the more difficult skills done by the world-class skaters who may have inspired them to start skating in the first place.

Training Tip

Chapters 4 through 9 contain exercises designed to help skaters master each skill more quickly. The exercises can be performed either off the ice or at the **rink barrier**. If the rink barrier is used, make certain the ice is of good quality and well groomed up to the barrier. If the ice is not safe, use a ballet barre or a similar device mounted to the floor off ice.

Stops

Learning the proper way to stop is just as important as learning how to glide gracefully across the ice. Holding the hands out in front and running head-on into the boards is not a good way to stop, and neither is dragging the toe to reduce speed and eventually come to a halt. The following are four effective methods of stopping.

Figure 4.1   Snowplow stop.

Snowplow Stop

The first and most basic stop is a snowplow (figure 4.1). When executing a snowplow stop, the feet start in a parallel position about shoulder-width apart. With just the right amount of pressure, both feet should press against the ice and slide out to the sides, ending in a V position—just like the plow on the front of a vehicle that removes snow. This stop, once learned, becomes a bridge to learning other stops. When new and more difficult stops are mastered, this stop is seldom used.

Teaching Tip

A fun exercise for children is called "Yikes! Stripes!" Have the kids practice snowplow stops on a painted hockey line on the ice, where the prints show up clearly. To help teach skaters what the right amount of pressure is, have them practice with one foot at a time by keeping their balance over one foot while the other foot is pushing out to the side. If they do this exercise correctly a bit of snow will be shaved from the ice and a **print** will show a skid mark.

T-Stop

A T-stop is named for the posi-tion of the feet at the end of the stop. In this position, the feet form an upside-down T: left foot in front, right foot behind, with the heel of the left foot placed to the instep of the right, as shown in figure 4.2. Both arms are stretched out to the side with the palms of the hands facing the ice and pressing down slightly. A slight lifting in the ribcage keeps the back straight to maintain good pos-ture, balance, and stability.

Beginners can learn to per-form the T-stop while moving forward on a one-footed glide. One foot is picked up and placed on the ice 12 to 18 inches behind the other in a perpen-dicular position. The front knee should be slightly bent with the back knee straight. The back foot pulls lightly toward

Figure 4.2   T-stop.

the front foot with a pressure similar to the pressure used in the snowplow stop. This drag pulls the body to a stop, ending with the feet in the T position. Both knees should be straight at the conclusion of the stop.

A T-stop is not the method to use for stopping quickly. It is a prepared stop that is controlled and aesthetically pleasing. Practice T-stops both with the right foot in front and with the left foot in front. After a while, try placing the back foot on an outside edge close behind the front foot. This helps develop subtle control of an outside edge, which is necessary in order to learn a one-foot stop.

> Stand facing the rink barrier and hold on with both hands. Practice making snow piles by placing the toe of the front foot perpendicular to the boards and drawing the back foot to the front. Repeat over and over on both feet. This exercise allows you to feel how much pressure you must apply to draw to a stop. As you become more proficient, you'll be able to apply a greater amount of pressure within a shorter amount of time.

Hockey Stop

The hockey stop, shown in figure 4.3, is the most advanced stop and the one most frequently used by both hockey and figure skaters. It's also the stop to use to avoid

Figure 4.3   Hockey stop.

another person or object on the ice when there's little time to "apply the brakes."

The hockey stop can be performed while gliding forward on two feet with the knees bent. The knees are raised and both feet are turned to the side, with the hips and shoulders held **square** to the print and the shoulders kept in a **checked** position. The body's weight should balance over a point slightly to the front of the center of the blade so that the blade can swing from a forward to a sideways position. (The feet will be at a 90-degree angle to the body when completely stopped.) As the feet turn, the knees bend rapidly so that force is applied to the ice to stop quickly. The arms remain straight out to the side during the entire stop. Practice this stop turning to both the right and left sides.

> To get a feel for the motion used in the hockey stop, practice twisting the body in place from right to left with the feet always working together and ending in the opposite direction from the shoulders and hips.

One-Footed Stop

Think of a hockey stop as a two-footed stop. A one-footed stop (figure 4.4) is a hockey stop done on just one foot turning to either the right or the left. The one-footed stop is a more showy stop; no one would use just one foot if the stop were urgent. It can be executed by lifting either the back or the front foot. It is a more advanced stop that should be learned only after mastering control of both outside and inside edges, which are described later in this chapter. The principles that apply in a one-footed hockey stop are identical to those in a two-footed stop. The turn of the foot and the shoulder and arm positions remain as executed in the two-footed hockey stop, which is why the two-footed hockey stop must be learned before the one-footed stop is attempted. The change in balance is identical to the change from a two-footed glide to a one-footed glide, which is also described later in this chapter.

Stroking Skills

Good stroking skills are an obvious necessity in figure skating. Stroking techniques are not just a means of getting from point A to point B. They connect steps to form

Figure 4.4   One-footed stop.

a routine, and they also provide the swift and controlled entrances and exits required for jumps and spins. Skaters who have mastered basic gliding and sculling skills can even add their own artistic touches, making stroking techniques just as important as the skills they lead into.

Forward Sculling

Sculling is a method of moving across the ice without having to lift either foot. It is a pump step that can be executed either forward or backward. For forward sculling, the feet start together in a V position with the toes pointed outward. Arms should be extended out to the side for good balance. Body weight should be kept on the blades slightly back of center, and the knees should be bent. This balance is maintained for all forward skating.

The inside edge of each foot is pressed to push the feet forward and out to the side until they are parallel and slightly more than shoulder-width apart. Then the knees straighten and the feet begin to pull back together, pointing the toes in until the feet are side by side again. Repeat this action—pointing the toes out and pushing out, then pulling in—over and over until the movement flows easily. Be patient. Practice, and just the right amount of pressure will lead to gliding forward gracefully and effortlessly.

Forward Glides

Basic stroking begins close to the boards until confidence grows and the barrier is no longer needed. Short steps are used to progress forward, and then both feet are kept on the ice while coasting. The body is balanced over both feet and the weight is placed slightly back of center on the blade.

Skaters who have mastered the two-footed glide can begin the one-footed glide, in which one foot (the free foot) lifts off the ice while the weight shifts over the other foot (the skating foot). For proper stroking, the feet begin in a parallel position about shoulder-width apart. The first stroke begins as both knees bend and one foot rotates simultaneously out to nearly a 45-degree angle (figure 4.5a). (Either the right or left foot can be chosen; the right foot is used here for illustrative purposes.) The right foot presses against the ice and pushes with the entire blade while the weight of the body transfers to the left foot and the body glides forward on one foot, as shown in figure 4.5b. Thus, the right foot provides the force to begin the forward movement and the left foot does the gliding. Most skaters should be able to glide a distance of three times their height. The move finishes by bringing both feet back together into the initial start position. Repeat the glide on the other foot.

Practice this exercise until it becomes one smooth and continuous motion. Glide forward on one foot and push with the other using the technique described earlier. Repeat this over and over on the same foot. This is called a one-footed pump step. Then repeat the entire exercise with the other foot. Complete the exercise by alternating each stroke with right foot, then left foot while moving forward across the ice.

a   b

Figure 4.5   Forward stroking: *(a)* The right foot presses against the ice to begin the forward movement, and *(b)* the left foot does the gliding.

Advanced Forward Stroking

Using greater knee and ankle bend to lengthen the stroke increases a skater's power and speed. The bend should increase before the stroke occurs. The primary push begins with the feet together. First, the ankle and knee bend forward, with the upper body straight and the back erect. Then the push-off leg straightens as the foot presses against the ice, propelling the skating (or strike-off) foot forward. As the push-off foot leaves the ice it becomes the free foot and is fully extended behind the skating foot with the knee turned out and the toe pointed. The push off must occur from the inside edge of the blade and not from the toe pick. The middle to the ball of the foot should press on the blade against the ice.

The secondary part of the push off is the straightening of the ankle as the body glides forward and the free leg is extended and stretched behind the skating foot. Next, the free leg lowers and is placed beside the skating foot with both knees bent, returning to the primary position with both feet together.

The entire stroke is repeated on the other foot. The bend, extension, and stretch are the elements that produce an advanced forward stroke.

Doing exercises is essential to increase the strength and power of each push you perform. A number of years ago champion skiers developed an excellent method for increasing lower extremity strength. Align your back against a solid wall. Your feet should be approximately 12 to 18 inches from the wall with the toes pointed forward. Very slowly lower your body until the thighs (quadriceps) are perpendicular to the wall. At that point stop lowering the body. Hold this position for 30 seconds before returning to a standing position. Keep the arms either folded across the chest or held out to the side. This exercise should be supervised by a trained professional to avoid undue stress.

Power Stroking

Power stroking enables a skater to accelerate quickly so as to reach a high rate of speed in the shortest amount of time. Power stroking is more than just quickly pushing into the ice. It is a means of explosive acceleration. The explosive push and pressure from the knee and ankle must be felt as the skating blade presses into and pushes away from the ice surface.

Stand on one of the hockey blue lines. Upon a signal from your coach, accelerate quickly to the mid- or red line. The time between the start of the acceleration and the crossing of the red line will decrease as the stroke becomes stronger.

Backward Sculling

Backward sculling uses the same basic movements as forward sculling. The feet start together, but this time the toes are pointed in and the heels out. The arms are stretched out to the side to maintain good balance. Just as in forward sculling, the weight on the blades is slightly forward of center and the knees are bent. This balance is maintained for all backward skating.

The backward movement starts as the inside edge of each foot is pressed, pushing the feet back and out to the side until they are parallel and slightly more than shoulder-width apart. Then the knees straighten and begin to pull the feet back together until they are side by side again. Repeat this push-pull pattern over and over until the movement flows smoothly. Keep practicing to find the right amount of pressure to move backward without getting stuck.

To practice the forward and backward sculling actions in place on the ice, stand with your feet directly under your body and twist the toes in and out to understand the foot and ankle actions. Add a little knee bend and some momentum forward or backward.

Backward Glides

Backward skating begins much the same as forward skating—close to the rink barrier and with short steps backward, with the toes pointed in and the heels turned out. (This is referred to as the backward "Duck Walk.") Skaters who have mastered this movement can progress to backward two-footed and one-footed glides. Body weight must be balanced forward over the ball of the foot—not on the toes—while skating backward.

Teaching Tip

Have skaters try a backward wiggle while standing on both feet. Tots can pretend they're bunnies wiggling through the carrot patch. With adults, suggest a hula hoop action.

Skaters who are comfortable making short backward steps are ready to try the backward two-footed glide. Moving backward gains speed to prepare for the glide, and then both feet are kept close together on the ice while coasting. The body is balanced over both feet and the weight is placed slightly forward of center on the blade.

After the backward two-footed glide has been mastered, the one-footed glide begins as one foot (the free foot) lifts off the ice while the weight shifts over the other (skating) foot. Skaters should practice on both feet until they can glide a distance of three times their height.

Advanced Backward Skating

Advanced backward skating begins by pushing from the right foot onto the left foot while skating backward. The right foot should be raised just above the ice. With the left knee slightly bent and the body weight remaining forward, the knee straightens slowly as the right foot comes beside the left. The movement is repeated to the other side, with the left foot lifting and coming beside the right. Balance is key: leaning too far back may cause a fall, but too far forward arrests the motion and puts a stop to the backward glide. For better backward skating, the free toe should point down and the head should look over one shoulder in the direction of the motion. The head should not face down.

Edges

Outside and inside edges are the foundation of figure skating and are necessary for developing good skating technique. Speed, balance, lean, and control are developed from strong edges. Without the development of these skills, skaters are limited in what they can perform. All beginning skaters should be introduced to edges early in their training even if they are not able to fully execute them. Practicing edges and improving edge quality is a lifelong endeavor.

There are two basic edges—outside and inside—but because a skater has two feet and can move either forward or backward, there are a total of eight combinations:

Outside—Right, left, forward, backward

Inside—Right, left, forward, backward

To understand the concept of edges, stand with both feet underneath you and slightly apart. Drop the left ankle to the outside. This is the left outside edge. Repeat with the other foot for the right outside edge. Now drop the left ankle to the inside. This is the left inside edge. Repeat with the other foot for the right inside edge. On the outside edges the little toe receives the greatest pressure. On the inside edges

The Art of Falling

It may seem strange to offer advice on how to fall. Falling is inevitable, however, and probably the greatest fear that a beginning skater encounters. That fear is compounded by age: the older the beginner, the greater the fear. If skaters feel comfortable with falling (and they will fall) then the learning process is easier and faster. That's why all coaches should begin their instruction to new skaters by teaching them to fall.

When a fall is about to occur there is no time to think about how to fall. It happens very quickly and without premeditation! Even the most accomplished skaters fall, however, and skaters who learn to relax and go with the fall have little chance of hurting themselves. Sliding with the ice can actually make falling fun.

A good way to fall is to slide to the side to avoid hitting the tailbone or the back of the head. It is difficult not to use the hands to break a fall, but it is best not to reach out as doing so may cause injury to the wrists. Fortunately, slight bruises or small cuts on the finger from sharp blades, although rare, are the most common injuries in skating.

Once a fall has occurred, it is often perplexing to determine how to get up. A good technique is to roll over onto all fours (hands and knees) and then draw the feet under the body as close as possible, using the hands in front to support the body weight. Pushing with the hands, slowly rise up on one foot and then the other until standing.

Teaching Tip

Always begin teaching new skaters by having them start seated on the ice. It is safer and less intimidating, especially if you're seated with them. On the first lesson, have your students practice sitting on the ice and getting up before giving any other instructions. It is practical to rehearse falling gently to get the feel of the ice and its slippery surface. Have your skaters practice this over and over to establish comfort and familiarity.

the big toe is pressed. Edges, which are always named for the foot, direction in which they begin, and edge (e.g., right forward outside), are always done one foot or direction at a time and always on a curve. The tighter the curve, the greater the edge.

Forward Outside Edges

The feet begin in a T position (right foot in front of the left, with the heel of the right foot placed to the instep of the left). Both arms should be stretched out to the side with the palms of the hands facing the ice and pressing down slightly. A slight lifting in the ribcage keeps the back straight. Both knees bend and the push off begins as the left ankle bends to the inside edge and the weight begins to transfer from both feet onto just the right foot. The body should lean slightly toward the right side, which produces an outside edge on a slight curve (figure 4.6). The left (free) side is held back and the left (free) foot is picked up and held behind the skating foot. The free foot then moves from behind, passing close beside the skating foot, ending in front and over the print, as shown in figure 4.6. The move should be repeated on the other foot, starting from the T position with the left foot in front, right foot behind.

Figure 4.6   Right forward outside edge.

A one-footed glide on a circle is a good way to introduce forward edges. Begin by skating forward on a circle, doing a pump step to gain speed and feel the forward outside edge. The foot that is on the inside of the circle will be on the outside edge. This exercise should be repeated in both directions to practice both right and left forward outside edges.

When executing any type of edge, it's important to keep the skating hip aligned with the ankle and shoulder. To practice this position, stand sideways with your left side facing the rink barrier at arm's length from the boards, standing on the left outside edge. Hold onto the barrier with your left hand. Keep the skating side aligned by checking three points: the ankle, the hip, and the shoulder. Make sure they form a straight, vertical line. Then, to feel the edge, bend and straighten the elbow of the arm that is holding onto the boards. Do not disturb the alignment of the ankle, hip, and shoulder, which starts as a vertical line but becomes diagonal as the elbow becomes more bent and the body is inclined toward the boards. Repeat this exercise several times on both feet.

Forward Inside Edges

For forward inside edges, the feet should start in a T position with the right foot in front and the left foot behind. The arm opposite to the skating foot—in this case, the left arm—is placed in front of the body with the palm of the hand facing the ice and pressing down slightly. The right arm is placed behind the body and on a plane level with the front (or left) arm. Both knees bend and the push off begins as the left ankle bends to the inside edge and the weight from both feet begins to transfer onto just the right foot. The body should lean slightly to the left, creating an inside edge on a slight curve (figure 4.7). The body is held square to the **tracing** while the left (free) side is held back and the left foot is picked up and held behind the skating foot. The free foot then moves from behind, passing close beside the skating foot, ending in front and over the print, as shown in figure 4.7. The exercise should be repeated on the other foot, starting with the left foot in front, right foot behind.

Figure 4.7   Right forward inside edge.

Training Tip

The proper starting position involves a slight lifting of the ribcage so that the back is straight. This helps maintain good posture, balance, and stability.

Glide on two feet on a circle. Pick up the foot that is to the inside of the circle. The remaining (skating) foot is on an inside edge. Practice the circles in both clockwise and counterclockwise directions.

Back Outside Edges

The feet begin in parallel position, shoulder-width apart. Arms should be out to the side with the palms facing the ice. Both knees bend. The knees are raised and the weight shifts from both feet onto just the left foot in order for the left foot to push onto the right back outside edge. As the weight is transferring, the right foot is picked up about three inches into the air and the toe is pointed inward, or pigeon-toed, so that when it is placed down on the ice it is on a backward rather than a forward edge. The backward momentum is gained by pushing off with the left foot, causing a print in the ice that is curved and often referred to as a "rat tail" because of its appearance. The right foot is on an outside edge and on a slight curve. The left (free) foot is then picked up and held above the skating foot and over the print. The left arm is in front and the right arm is behind. This move should be repeated on the other foot, starting from the parallel position and transferring the weight from the right foot to the left.

Doing a backward one-footed glide on a circle is an effective way to learn back edges. Start by skating backward on a circle, doing a pump step to gain speed. Feel the back outside edge. The foot that is on the inside of the circle will be on the outside edge. Practice skating circles both clockwise and counterclockwise.

Back Inside Edges

The feet are placed parallel to each other and shoulder-width apart. Arms are stretched out to the side. Both knees bend and the weight transfers from both feet onto just the left foot in order to push with the left foot onto the right back inside edge. As the weight shifts, the right foot rises about three inches into the air and the toe points inward. When the foot is placed back on the ice, it is on a backward rather than a forward edge. Backward momentum is gained as the left foot pushes off, causing a curved print in the ice. The right foot is on an inside edge and on a slight curve. The left (free) foot is then lifted and held above the skating foot and over the print. The left arm is in front and the right arm is behind the body. The move should be repeated on the other foot, starting from the parallel position and transferring the weight from the right foot to the left.

Glide backward on two feet on a circle. Pick up the foot that is to the inside of the circle, and the remaining (skating) foot is on an inside edge. Practice moving both clockwise and counterclockwise.

Change of Edge

A change of edge can be done from any edge on either foot and in either direction. The print on the ice looks like an S or serpentine pattern. It is a rocking movement from one edge to another. The change of edge is used when a skater on one foot wishes to change edges without placing the other foot on the ice. Examples are one-footed sculling, the changing of an edge before a turn, and an entrance variation into a jump or spin. The change of edge is also an important skill to learn to quickly recover when slightly off balance.

Forward Outside to Inside Change of Edge

A right forward outside to inside (RFOI) change begins on a curve on the right forward outside (RFO) edge with the left (free) foot behind and over the print, the right arm in front, and the left arm behind (figure 4.8a). The left foot comes forward while the left shoulder presses back (figure 4.8b). The curve straightens out to a flat (the middle part of the S), allowing the outside edge to become an inside edge while the left foot moves back (figure 4.8c). The change should be practiced on the left foot as well as the right.

A common mistake in a change of edge is to overrotate the shoulders going into the change so that it is impossible to reverse the position and change to the other edge. Another common mistake is to break the alignment of the skating hip, which also makes it impossible to move from one edge to the other.

a

b

Figure 4.8 Forward outside to inside change of edge: *(a)* Start on a right outside edge, then *(b)* bring the left foot forward, so that *(c)* the right foot can change to an inside edge.

c

When executing a change of edge, always keep the weight and lean of the body over the skating hip.

Forward Inside to Outside Change of Edge

The change from a right forward inside to outside edge (RFIO) is executed in the same manner as the forward outside to inside change of edge. It begins on a curve on the right forward inside (RFI) edge with the left (free) foot behind and over the print, the left arm in front, and the right arm behind. The left foot is brought forward while the right shoulder presses back. As the curve straightens out, the inside edge becomes an outside edge and the left foot is brought back. The arms do not change. This change of edge must be practiced on the left foot as well as the right. If done correctly the change will be very subtle and the flat line very short.

Edges should never be done by "ankle" skating, but it is helpful to practice the feel of the change by exaggerating the action of the ankle from outside to inside while standing on two feet and pressing on a strong outside and then a strong inside edge, one foot at a time.

Backward Outside to Inside Change of Edge

The right backward outside to inside (RBOI) change begins on a curve on the right back outside (RBO) edge with the left (free) foot in front and over the print, the left arm in front, the right arm behind, and the head looking into the curve of the circle. The left foot moves back while the right shoulder presses back. The curve straightens out to a flat, letting the outside edge become an inside edge while the left foot moves forward and the head turns to the inside of the new curve with no change to the arms. The skill should be practiced on both feet.

Backward Inside to Outside Change of Edge

The execution of the right backward inside to outside change (RBIO) is much like that of the backward outside to inside edge. It begins on a curve on the right back inside (RBI) edge with the left (free) foot in front and over the print, the left arm in front, the right arm behind, and the head looking into the curve of the circle. The left foot moves back while the right shoulder presses back. The change begins as the left arm drops down, passes close by the body, and then lifts so that it is leading and the right arm is trailing as the curve straightens out to a flat, allowing the inside edge to become an outside edge. Then the left foot moves forward. The head does not turn but continues to look outside the curve of the circle. Changes on the left foot as well as the right should be practiced.

The backward change of edge should be practiced on two feet before it is tried on one foot. Practicing on two feet is a good training technique in that it allows the brain to concentrate on body positions without having to worry about balance.

In an advanced change of edge, the change or flat part of the S should be no more than one foot long.

Crossovers

Crossovers are necessary to round a corner with good flow and control. In this technique one foot crosses over the other in a smooth and powerful maneuver. Crossovers can be done in both clockwise and counterclockwise directions and can be executed on both feet.

Forward Crossovers

Forward crossovers are executed by using both outside and inside edges while alternating feet and moving forward on a circle. This technique can be understood by skating clockwise and stepping or crossing one foot over the other. Adding some speed and a lean into the circle places the skates on an edge. With the weight on the outside edge of the left foot (figure 4.9a), the right foot crosses over on an inside edge (figure 4.9b). The right arm should be in front and the left arm out to the side so that if the arms were the hands on a clock the time would read 3:00. Next, the left foot is picked up and placed beside the right one. The process is repeated. The arms should not change position throughout the crossover whether the weight is on the right or left foot. The skill should be repeated going the opposite direction on a counterclockwise circle.

a   b

Figure 4.9   Forward crossovers: *(a)* With the weight on the outside edge of the left foot, *(b)* the right foot crosses over on an inside edge.

Begin by standing in place with both feet close together. Pick up the left foot and place it on the ice crossing it in front of the right. Pick up the right foot and place it back beside the left in the original, or neutral, position. Repeat this exercise, stepping sideways across the ice over and over in the same direction until your balance is secure. Repeat back to the other side, crossing the right foot over the left. Also practice a forward pump step on a circle. Do not lift up either foot but practice skating forward in both a clockwise and counterclockwise direction.

Training Tip

To make forward crossovers more advanced, each step should become a stroke and, with practice, speed should be added to make this a powerful means of moving forward on a circle or traversing the end of the rink. The alternating skating knee should always be bent and the free leg should always be straight and extended. Push from the blade, not the toe picks.

Back Crossovers

Back crossovers are the most common and powerful means of skating backward. Both the outside and inside edges are used while the feet alternate and the body moves backward on a circle.

The technique is the same as for forward crossovers except that the direction of movement is reversed. When the weight is on the outside edge of the left foot while skating backward on a circle in a clockwise direction, the right foot crosses over in front on an inside edge. The right arm is in front and the left arm extended in the direction of travel. Next, the left foot is raised and placed beside the right. The move is repeated by once again crossing the right foot over the left. The arms should not change position throughout the crossover whether the weight is on the right or left foot. The back crossover must also be practiced going the opposite direction on a counterclockwise circle.

Just as in forward crossovers, the skating knee is bent and the free leg straight and extended. To build power, the inside foot is placed into the circle and the feet are drawn together before the outside foot is picked up and crossed over again. As technique improves, the front foot is left on the ice while only the back foot is picked up and placed into the circle, providing a scissor action that increases power and speed. Back crossovers should be executed smoothly, using edge pressure and knee bend to enhance technique.

Practice a backward pump step on a circle. Do not lift up either foot but practice skating backward in both a clockwise and counterclockwise direction. When your balance is secure, practice picking up and stepping one foot over the other with little backward momentum. When these skills are mastered, add speed.

Summary

The skills introduced in this chapter make up the cornerstone of figure skating. It's important to take the time to become proficient at these basics now, since they play a part in all of the skills that come later. The ability to master more difficult techniques will depend largely on how well these fundamentals are performed. Skaters who have a good handle on the basics and can execute them well and without much thought can move onto bigger and better things in the following chapters!

chapter 5
Freestyle Moves

Freestyle moves can and must be integrated into the process of learning the basics. It is unlikely that a skater will remain interested in the sport if the joy of performing a simple jump or spin is not added to the learning process. The progression is much the same as with music: technique and scales are important, but the ability to play a simple tune is such great fun that the incentive to learn deepens. In skating, spirals, bunny hops, and two-footed spins can be introduced during the first few weeks of instruction. The skater's fun and pride in being able to show off a new skill is more important than the proficiency of the technique.

Artistic moves incorporate all the steps between the jumps, spins, and footwork. The imagination is the only limit to the number of artistic moves that can be created. The basics include spirals, lunges, shoot-the-ducks, pivots, spread eagles, and Bauers.

Spirals

In ballet a spiral is called an *arabesque*. When done well it is one of the most beautiful moves in skating. It requires flexibility, balance, and control. As with all skills, a spiral can be performed adequately with good extension, an arched back, and some flexibility. Skaters like Nicole Bobek and Michelle Kwan perform them masterfully. Their extraordinary stretch and artistic application have turned a simple artistic move into an awesome one.

Forward Spiral

After a good one-footed glide has been developed a spiral can be taught, starting from a forward two-footed glide. The arms are held out to the side, and the waist bends forward to a 90-degree angle from the legs. The back should be arched. Then one leg slowly lifts while the body stays balanced over the back of the blade. (See figure 5.1.) A beginning goal is to lift the leg so that it is parallel with the torso.

Tom Zakrajsek, coach of U.S. Junior Men's Champion Ryan Bradley, describes the body in a spiral as being in a "banana position," with the curve from the foot to the head resembling that of a banana. The more the body leans forward, the more the weight is pushed backward on the blade and the more the back becomes arched. Spirals should be practiced on each foot.

Once a skater has good balance and control in a straight line, the forward spiral can be learned on both edges—inside and outside. It can be started from forward stroking or, as an advanced move, be done with a crossover or change of edge. Flexibility is key. When control in the spiral has been mastered, the free leg should be raised higher and higher while the chest remains parallel to the ice. Skaters who do not have mirrors available on the ice can check their reflection in the Plexiglas to ensure that their legs are straight and their backs are properly arched.

Off-ice stretching is important for all skaters. Stretching is for the back, the neck, the shoulders and arms, the hips, and the legs. Using a ballet barre is helpful. Place one leg on the barre. Keeping both legs straight and the knees locked with the hip turned out, lean forward and try to touch your forehead to the knee on the barre. Next, turn slightly away from the barre, keeping one leg elevated, and try touching your forehead to the knee of the standing leg. Reverse and do the same exercises with the other leg on the barre.

Figure 5.1   Forward spiral.

Next, sit on the floor and spread your legs as far apart as possible, keeping your back arched. Lean forward, grab one leg with both hands, and touch your head first to one leg and then the other. When you are warmed up and sufficiently stretched out, practice the splits as well. Never overstretch, risking a pulled muscle. Stretch to the point of resistance and then remain in that position for about five to seven seconds before releasing. Never push beyond this point or pump to try to extend farther.

Back Spiral

With the arms held out to the sides for balance, a back spiral begins from a backward one-footed glide. The waist bends forward until the torso becomes parallel to the ice as one leg slowly lifts. The body weight should balance over the front of the blade and the back should be arched. The more the body leans forward, the more the weight is pushed toward the front of the blade and the more the back arches. Back spirals should be practiced on both feet. It is extremely important to look around before beginning this move to make sure the ice is clear and there's no likelihood of running into another skater.

Once a skater has good balance and control in a straight line the back spiral, like the forward spiral, can be performed on both outside and inside edges. It can be started from back crossovers or, as an advanced move, it can be done with a change of edge. Flexibility is again key. Once control has been gained in the spiral, the free leg should be raised higher and higher.

Use the same off-ice stretching exercises for both the forward and backward spirals. Practicing back bends is also useful for developing strong back muscles. Stand on two feet, facing close to the ballet barre and holding on with both hands. Lean back away from the barre, lifting up through the ribcage while pressing your hips slightly toward the barre. When fully stretched, work with a spotter to practice a back bend away from the barre. Standing on two feet with your hands extended above your head, lean back until both hands are resting on the floor and your back forms a bridge from hands to feet.

Lunges and Shoot-the-Ducks

Lunges and shoot-the-ducks add fun and new skills to a beginner's skating accomplishments. A lunge can be used as a stand-alone move or as a variation on the entrance or exit of a spin or jump, while a shoot-the-duck aids in the muscular development and balance needed later for sit spins. Both of these freestyle moves can be made more interesting by adding creative arm movements or by reversing the direction and performing them while skating backward.

Lunge

A lunge is done by bending the skating knee fully, stretching the free leg behind it, and drawing the free leg on the ice behind the skating foot. A lunge can begin from a forward two-footed glide. The right foot is picked up and the leg is turned out to an open position, but the hips stay square. The left leg begins to bend at the knee. When the right foot touches the ice it must not catch the blade. Instead, the side of the boot is placed on the ice by pointing the toes up and arching the foot. The left knee continues to bend to a fully bent position with the free leg fully extended behind the torso on the ice. The head should be up and the arms should be stretched out to the side.

In rising up from a lunge, the torso leans slightly more forward over the skating foot while at the same time the right foot lifts from the ice. The arms remain out to the side, and the move finishes in a two-footed forward glide. Lunges should be practiced on both feet. Backward lunges can also be attempted using extreme caution when placing the foot on the ice so that the boot, not the blade, touches the ice.

Shoot-the-Duck

A shoot-the-duck is executed by bending fully on the skating knee and stretching the free foot directly out in front while moving in a straight line (figure 5.2). The skills for a shoot-the-duck can be developed by adding a dip to a forward two-footed glide, lowering the body until both knees are fully bent. The weight should start toward the back of the blade but push forward as the body is lowered to keep a center of balance. The arms should be kept out in front.

Figure 5.2   Shoot-the-duck.

Once a dip and a forward one-footed glide have been mastered, a shoot-the-duck can be learned. It begins with a one-footed glide with the free foot in front. The body lowers, pushing proportionately forward on the blade. The arms can hold on to the extended free foot or knee for balance, but an advanced exercise is to keep the arms out to the side, which requires a great deal more strength. To rise up from a shoot-the-duck, the torso leans forward and the body rises slowly over the skating leg. This skill should be developed on both feet, both edges, and both directions.

The most important exercise for skills like the lunge and the shoot-the-duck is one that develops the muscles necessary to bend and rise on one leg. This increased strength can be developed through supervised off-ice conditioning as described in chapter 3 or through practicing the bending and rising position at the boards, being careful to keep the weight forward. Repeat this exercise no more than two or three times on each foot at first, being careful not to overexert the muscles or cause muscle strain.

Pivots

A pivot is a pretty move from the spin family. It positions the toe of one foot on the ice while the other foot circles around it on an edge. In addition to being a movement on its own, the pivot can also serve as an entrance into or exit from a spin.

Figure 5.3   Forward inside pivot.

Figure 5.4   Forward outside pivot.

Forward Inside Pivot

The simplest of all the pivots, the forward inside pivot can be done on either the right or the left foot and in a forward or backward direction. It is begun by skating slowly forward on a small counterclockwise curve on the right inside edge. The left (free) foot should be placed inside the circle with the arms out to the side. The toe pick of the left foot is placed gently into the ice. The left knee bends and the right foot continues around the left leg counterclockwise on the inside edge (figure 5.3). The weight over the left toe increases until the knee reaches a deep bend (or lunge position) while the right leg remains straight and pivots around the left toe. The right and left feet should begin the pivot close together, but the right foot spirals away from the left as the rotations on the pivot increase. The feet draw back together and the left knee straightens before the pivot is exited. This pivot should be practiced on the other foot as well, using a clockwise rotation. A mini-pivot may also be used as an entrance into a two-footed spin.

Forward Outside Pivot

A forward outside pivot is entered from a forward outside edge on either foot. The toe of the free foot is placed into the center of the circle and the weight of the body is placed over the skating toe while the foot travels in a circle around the skating toe (figure 5.4). The knees must stay together to keep the body balanced over the skating toe. The arms should be extended out to the sides at first but may be varied once this difficult pivot is mastered. This pivot is very difficult and seldom used.

Back Inside Pivot

Preparation for the back inside pivot, as well as for the forward inside pivot, may begin with the toe of one foot placed in the ice while the blade of the second foot pushes away in an ever-increasing circle around the toe that is stationary on the ice. For a right back inside pivot, the right toe is placed in the ice, the left arm is held in front of the body, and the right arm is held behind. The left foot pushes against the ice on a back inside edge in a spiraling counterclockwise circle around the right toe. The right knee should be bent and the left knee straight (as in a lunge position) with the body weight kept over the right toe. When the pivot is exited, the circle made by the left foot is tightened by drawing the foot in closer to the right toe until both feet are side by side in a two-footed spin. This pivot should also be practiced on the left foot in a clockwise rotation.

Training Tip

Do not try to turn on the pivot too early or place the toe into the ice too quickly or forcefully. It is a matter of touch. Practice placing the toe on the ice until you understand and can control the toe's placement and the positioning of the body weight over the toe.

Back Outside Pivot

The back outside pivot is quite difficult. It should begin slowly and then, when mastered, be executed with great speed to become a spectacular move. It is used in many freestyle programs and can easily be combined with spins. It is commonly used in pair skating, where it is the man's position in a death spiral.

Figure 5.5   Back outside pivot.

Entry into the pivot begins on a left back outside edge. The toe of the right foot scrapes slightly across the ice and inside the tracing made by the left foot. The right knee must be placed back inside the circle as well. The right toe is then planted firmly into the ice, and the left foot continues in a circle around the right toe in a counterclockwise rotation. (See figure 5.5.) The left leg is straight and the right knee is well bent. The arms are out to the sides of the body. After several rotations, the pivot is exited by circling the right foot closer to the left until the right knee is straight and the body weight is balanced over both feet in a two-footed spin position. The back outside pivot should also be practiced in a clockwise rotation on the right foot.

When mastered, the pivot is executed in a fast sweeping movement across the ice on the back outside edge, with the toe of the free foot dragging behind and the knee of the free leg bent well back into the circle. As the circle grows smaller and the toe can be placed firmly on the ice, the pivot can be held for several rotations before exiting or stopping in place.

Practice only the back outside edge entrance into the pivot, holding the toe of the free foot off the ice as long as possible to gain control and balance over the edge.

Spread Eagle

Not every skater can perform this move, which depends on the ability to open the hips. It can be done by both men and women and, when executed well, it is a dramatic skating move. In ballet it is the *second position*.

Inside Spread Eagle

The inside spread eagle is begun by starting on the left forward inside edge and swinging the right (free) foot forward past the left (skating) foot. Then the right leg swings back and the right foot is placed on the ice about 12 to 18 inches behind the left foot on the same curve on a back inside edge. (See figure 5.6.) This move requires an open hip position. Both knees must be straight and locked, the back must be arched, and the arms should be extended out to the sides. Practice spread eagles on both the right and left feet. Experiment with creative arm positions.

Figure 5.6   Inside spread eagle.

Master the Move

Paul Wylie's Signature Skill: The Spread Eagle

Photo courtesy of Monica Freidlander

Paul Wylie's flawless technique and expression in this inside spread eagle help enhance the emotion in his dramatic programs.

The spread eagle is one of Paul Wylie's signature moves. It's his impeccable technique—the strongly arched back and extended arms—and his overall carriage and expression that make his spread eagle a particularly classy move.

Known for his dramatic programs and breathtaking artistry, Wylie uses moves like the spread eagle to complement and enhance the emotion projected throughout his performances. He even adds to the level of difficulty by performing inside and outside spread eagles in a continuous pattern down the ice. By adding another element to his spread eagle, he managed to do what all great skaters do: He turned something ordinary into the extraordinary.

To emulate Wylie's technique, you'll need to develop an open hip position. Exercises that stretch out the hips and legs are a good place to start. Facing the rink barrier, hold on with both hands. Stretch your legs out in opposite directions, keeping the instep of each foot braced against the barrier. Press your hips against the barrier and lean back slightly, arching the back. This exercise replicates the action on the ice away from the barrier and stretches out the hips and legs. The barrier also acts as a resistance, helping to stretch open the hips.

After you've developed the ability to open the hips and have mastered the spread eagle, practice alternating outside and inside spread eagles in a serpentine pattern down the ice. This dramatic and difficult maneuver combines the change of edge described in chapter 4 with the spread eagle position. The key is to lift the body slightly before each change to reduce the friction on the ice when changing from one edge to the other.

Outside Spread Eagle

The outside spread eagle is begun by stroking forward to gain speed. A left forward outside spread eagle starts on the left forward outside edge and uses the same swinging motion of the right (free) foot as on the inside spread eagle, except that both feet are on outside rather than inside edges. (See figure 5.7.) This move requires an extremely open hip position. Both knees must be straight and locked, the back must be arched, and the arms must be extended out to the side. Once this move has been mastered the outside spread eagle can be entered from back crossovers, holding the right back outside edge and rotating the body around so that the left foot can be placed on the ice without doing the forward swing. Outside spread eagles should be practiced on both feet. Experiment with creative arm positions.

Figure 5.7   Outside spread eagle.

The Bauer

This dramatic move is named for its originator, Ina Bauer, German champion from 1956 to 1960. A variation of the spread eagle, it requires that the skater bend the front knee while keeping the back knee straight. It is frequently referred to as the *Bauer*.

This move is most easily executed from back crossovers. For a Bauer with the right foot in front, the left back inside edge is held as the right foot is placed on the ice on a forward outside edge. The left foot remains on a back inside edge. The upper body is arched. The Bauer can be dramatically performed in a layback position with the arms overhead or out to the side, as shown in figure 5.8.

The equalized balance and edge pressure between the front and back legs allows movement in a straight line across the ice. The Bauer is usually done on a diagonal from one corner of the rink to the other. It can also be executed on a strong outside edge, allowing movement forward on an outside edge circle, or with both the front and back feet on a forward inside edge, producing movement in an inside edge circle.

Figure 5.8   The Bauer.

Flexibility, muscular strength, and control are key to executing this move. Splits, laybacks, and exercises that develop strength in the quads and hamstrings, such as pliés and lunges, are necessary for a good Bauer.

Summary

Freestyle moves add interest and variety to skating routines and can be creatively varied with innovative arm and leg positions. These are skills that nearly every skater can learn, from tot to adult, and though not everyone will be able to turn multirevolutions in the air, skaters can achieve artistry in every performance by including these moves.

chapter 6
Turns and Footwork

In the past all turns were learned on circles and executed as a part of compulsory figures. In 1990 figures were removed from international competition, and eight years later they were removed in the United States from qualifying competitions. A new format was devised, not to replace figures but to teach and train the discipline necessary to execute turns in freestyle and dance. The new format, named Moves in the Field, incorporates turns used in freestyle and dance in a series of tests prescribed by the United Figure Skating Association, but it does not require the precision that was formerly demanded in compulsory figures.

This chapter describes every basic turn performed in skating, including three turns, Mohawks, Choctaws, brackets, rockers, and counters. Each turn is done on both feet and in both the forward and backward directions. Every move in skating incorporates these turns to connect steps, to enter a jump or spin, or especially to perform footwork. Footwork is simply a combination of turns and freestyle moves. You'll learn the components of good footwork that, when combined with creativity and personality, make a good program great.

Three Turns

A three turn is done on one foot on a curve to change direction 180 degrees, from front to back or from back to front. The turn gets its name from the pattern made on the ice, which resembles the numeral 3. (See figure 6.1.) A three turn changes edge and direction, but it does not involve changing feet: A turn that begins on an outside edge ends on an inside edge, and a turn that begins on an inside edge ends on an outside edge. If the turn begins in a forward direction, it ends in a backward direction. The same foot, however, is used throughout the turn. As with edges, threes are named for the edge, foot, and direction in which they begin, with eight turns designated by foot (right or left), direction (forward or backward), and edge (outside or inside).

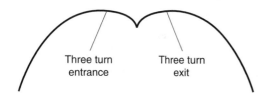

Three turn entrance

Three turn exit

Figure 6.1 The pattern on the ice left by a three turn.

Forward Outside Three

A right forward outside three begins on the right foot, moving forward on an outside edge. It ends on a right back inside edge.

PREPARATION

While the turn is being learned, the arms may begin in the same position as for an outside edge or they may already be rotated so that the left arm is forward and the right arm back. The continued rotation of the arms around the body begins the rotation of the upper body (from the waist up, not including the hips) over the skating foot. Because this is a forward edge, the body is balanced just back of the center part of the blade. The left (free) foot remains behind the skating foot over the tracing.

This chapter was written by Carole Shulman and reviewed by Sandy Lamb. Lamb has been teaching skating for 34 years and is a level VI ranked coach. She holds a master rating in dance and free dance, group skating, and program administration, and holds additional ratings in Moves in the Field and freestyle. She has coached Regional to Olympic and World competitors. She has been the figure skating director for Special Olympics International since 1985.

TURN

Because the movement is on a curve to begin with, the circle becomes tighter as the arms rotate, increasing the pressure between the shoulders and hips. The balance of the body over the blade begins to shift forward to just behind the first toe pick, causing the back of the blade to lift slightly to free the blade from scraping the ice during the turn. At the **apex** of the turn, the pressure on the hips is released as the arms change from the rotated position on entry to a checked position on the exit. In other words, at the top of the turn the arms and shoulders change from rotation to check, but the pressure is momentarily decreased as the arms change and the blade is pressed forward to help turn the foot from forward to backward, changing both direction and edge. A strong checked position maintains control after the turn. The free foot remains behind and to the heel of the skating foot throughout the entire turn. The knee is bent on entry, raised on the turn, and bent again on the exit.

Figure 6.1 illustrates the shape of the 3 and shows how the turn actually leaves the circle upon entry and returns to the circle upon completion. If a three is perfectly turned the entry and exit edges are symmetrical with no variations or subordinate curves. The preparation and turn should be repeated on the left foot for a left forward outside three.

Face the rink barrier, holding on with both hands, and practice turning and lifting the foot to feel the subtleties of change of balance and direction before trying to execute the turn away from the barrier. Also, begin by using two-footed turns on a circle before attempting a one-footed turn. This is an effective exercise for all types of three turns—forward and backward, inside and outside.

Forward Inside Three

A right forward inside three begins on the right foot, moving forward on an inside edge. It ends on a right back outside edge.

PREPARATION

When this turn is being learned, the arms may begin in the same position as for an inside edge or they may already be rotated so that the right arm is forward and the left arm is back. The rotation, turn, check, print, and exercises are the same as for forward outside threes.

TURN

The circle becomes tighter as the arms rotate, increasing the pressure between the shoulders and hips. The balance of the body over the blade begins to shift forward to just behind the first toe pick causing the back of the blade to lift slightly in order to free the blade from scraping the ice during the turn. At the apex of the turn, the pressure on the hips is released as the arms change from the rotated position upon entry to a checked position on the exit. In other words, at the top of the turn, the arms and shoulders change from rotation to check but the pressure is momentarily decreased as the arms change and the blade is pressed forward to assist in turning the foot from forward to backward, changing both direction and edge. A strong checked position maintains control after the turn.

The free foot remains behind and to the heel of the skating foot throughout the entire turn. The knee action is bent on the entry, raised on the turn and bent again on the exit. Repeat on the left foot for a left forward inside three.

Back Outside Three

A right back outside three turn begins on the right foot, moving backward on an outside edge. It ends on a right forward inside edge.

PREPARATION

To begin the turn, the arms are placed in the same position as for a back outside edge with the right arm leading, the left arm trailing, and the left (free) foot in front of the right (skating) foot and over the print. The head should be looking over the right shoulder. The rotation of the turn begins as the arms drop down and pass close by the body, then lift so that the left arm is leading and the right arm trailing. The head changes from looking over the right shoulder to looking over the left shoulder. The rotation of the arms and head along with the upper body (from the waist up, not including the hips) initiates the rotation into the turn. During this rotation, the body weight must be continuously maintained over the skating hip. Because this is a back edge, the body is balanced just forward of the center part of the blade. The placement of the free foot is optional; it can remain in front throughout the turn or move behind the skating foot before the turn. If the free foot is brought back it should move before the arms and head begin to rotate, passing close by the skating foot with the toe placed to the heel of the skating foot going into the turn.

TURN

As with forward threes, the circle becomes tighter as the arms rotate, increasing the pressure between the shoulders and hips. The balance of the body begins to shift back on the blade to just back of center, causing the toe to lift slightly to free the blade from scraping the ice during the turn. At the same time, the free foot lifts to help move the weight to the back of the blade as the turn is made. At the apex of the turn the pressure on the hips is momentarily released as the arms change from the rotated position upon entry to a checked position on the exit. In other words, just as with forward threes the arms and shoulders change from rotation to check at the top of the turn, but the pressure is momentarily decreased as the arms change and the blade lifts back toward the heel to help turn the foot from backward to forward, changing both direction and edge. A strong checked position maintains control after the turn. The free foot is in front and over the print on the exit of the turn. (If the free foot was brought back on the entry, it should snap forward at the top of the turn so that it is in front on the exit.) The knee is bent on the entry, raised on the turn, and bent again on the exit.

A left back outside three should be performed next by repeating this process on the left foot.

Back Inside Three

A right back inside three begins on the right foot, moving backward on an inside edge. It ends on a right forward outside edge.

PREPARATION

As the turn is approached the arm position is the same as for an inside edge, with the right arm back, the left arm forward, and the left (free) foot forward over the print. The head should be looking over the right shoulder. The continued rotation of the arms around the body begins the rotation of the upper body (from the waist up, not including the hips) over the skating foot. During this rotation the body weight should remain continuously over the skating hip. Because this is a back edge, the body is balanced just forward of the center part of the blade. The placement of the free foot is optional. It can remain in front and slightly pigeon-toed (or turned in) throughout the turn, or it can be placed behind the skating foot before the turn. If the foot is brought back it should pass close by the skating foot, placing the toe of the free foot to the heel of the skating foot going into the turn.

TURN

As the skater is on a curve to begin with, the circle becomes tighter as the arms rotate, increasing the pressure between the shoulders and hips. The balance of the body begins to shift back on the blade to just back of center causing the toe to lift slightly in order to free the blade from scraping the ice during the turn. At the same time, there is a lifting action with the free foot assisting in the movement of the weight to the back of the blade as the turn is made. At the apex of the turn, the pressure on the hips is released as the arms change from the rotated position upon entry to a checked position on the exit. In other words, at the top of the turn, the arms and shoulders change from rotation to check, the hip remains the same but the pressure is momentarily decreased as the arms change and the blade lifts up to assist in turning the foot from backward to forward, changing both direction and edge. A strong checked position maintains control after the turn. The free foot is in front and over the print on the exit of the turn. If the free foot has been brought back on the entry, it should snap forward at the top of the turn so that it is in front on the exit. The knee action is bent on the entry, raised on the turn and bent again on the exit. Repeat on the left foot for a left backward inside three.

Teaching Tip

If the free foot remains in front throughout the turn, tell the skater to "sweep the rainbow" as the three is turned. In this excellent visualization technique the skater pictures the arc of a rainbow and envisions the free foot sweeping from the beginning to the end of the rainbow.

Double Three

Double threes are a combination of forward and backward (or backward and forward) threes that are executed without putting the free foot down between the turns. A right forward outside three, for example, ends on a right back inside edge, which then becomes the edge that begins the second turn, a right back inside three. The second turn ends on a right forward outside edge—the same edge where the double three began.

Double threes can begin on either the right or the left foot, on either the outside or the inside edge, from either a forward or a backward direction. The skill that must be developed is the control of rotation between the turns. It is important to check the exit of the first three before beginning to rotate into the second one.

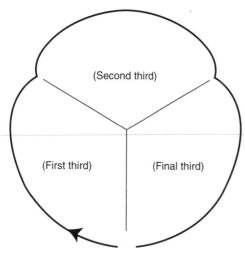

Figure 6.2   Double three on a circle.

Double threes are best practiced on a circle as in compulsory figures and then transferred to freestyle in the context in which they will be performed. On a circle, they should be placed in equal thirds around the circle, as shown in figure 6.2. (If you compare the circle to a clock and you begin at the six, then the double threes should be turned at ten and two.) If the threes are executed correctly on the circle they will point directly toward the middle of the circle, forming a Y in relation to the center.

Training Tip

Practice double threes on two feet before trying them on one foot. If you experience trouble checking and controlling rotation between turns, practice the double threes on a straight line before placing them back on a circle.

Drop Three

Drop three is a term used only in ice dancing to describe a particular step. A drop three is basically a three with an added step. It's a forward outside three that brings the feet immediately together at the point of three (but without putting the free foot on the ice). Both knees bend following the three, and then the new skating foot is placed on a back outside edge by pushing off from the foot that executed the three. In simple terms, it is a three with a step following the turn, and it is added to specific dance patterns. Sometimes it is used in a exercise involving multiple threes in a circle.

Mohawks

A Mohawk is another method of turning from front to back or vice-versa while traveling across the ice. The Mohawk is a two-footed turn as opposed to the one-footed three turn. Other differences between the Mohawk and three turn are listed in table 6.1. Like a three, it is executed on a curve, but it involves changing from one foot to the other. It changes direction but not edge. In most cases, unless it is specifically prescribed in a test, three turns and Mohawks can be interchanged when used as an entrance into another move.

As with edges and threes, there are eight Mohawks designated by foot (right or left), direction (forward or backward), and edge (outside or inside). By far the most common and most recognized are the forward turns. A Mohawk that begins on an inside edge involves a change of feet and direction but not edge. Mohawks can be executed as open or closed.

Table 6.1   Comparison Between Three Turns and Mohawks

	Change feet	Change edge	Change direction
Threes	No	Yes	Yes
Mohawks	Yes	No	Yes

The open or closed position is indicated by the position of the hip and free foot at the exit and by the placement of the free foot in relation to the skating foot. The different positions for the open and closed Mohawks are listed in table 6.2. With an open Mohawk, the heel of the free foot is placed at the instep of the skating foot ("heel to instep") and the hips are open at the exit. On a closed Mohawk the free foot is placed behind the heel of the skating foot ("instep to heel") and the hips are closed at the exit.

Table 6.2   Comparison of Open and Closed Mohawks

	Free foot placement	Finished position
Open	Brought to instep of skating foot	Free foot behind (or open)
Closed	Brought to heel of skating foot	Free foot forward (or closed)

Inside Open Mohawk

A right forward inside open Mohawk begins on the right foot, moving forward on an inside edge. It ends on the left back inside edge.

PREPARATION

The right forward inside Mohawk begins on a right forward inside edge on a well-bent knee with the left (free) foot behind (figure 6.3a), the right arm in front of the body, and the left arm in back. The right hip leads into the turn.

TURN

The skating knee begins to straighten as the left heel is brought to the instep of the right foot (figure 6.3b). The shoulders rotate into the turn just as in a three. The left foot is placed on the ice with the weight toward the ball of the foot, being careful not to step on the right blade. The weight shifts from the right (skating) foot to the left (new skating foot) as the left foot steps down on the ice on a bent knee on the left back inside edge (figure 6.3c). The shoulders, which rotated into the turn on the entry, tighten to a checked position on the exit to hold and maintain the back edge. The free foot and free arm are held back and open in the direction of travel.

The preparation and turn should be repeated beginning on the left foot to execute a left forward inside Mohawk.

Facing the rink barrier and holding on with both hands, stand heel to heel and step from the right forward inside edge to the left back inside edge. As this position becomes more comfortable, practice stepping heel to instep. Repeat several times from right to left and then left to right. Away from the barrier, practice a right forward inside edge, then step into a spread eagle position on two feet before picking up the right foot while remaining on a left back inside edge. This will help you feel the open hip position, which is necessary to execute a good Mohawk.

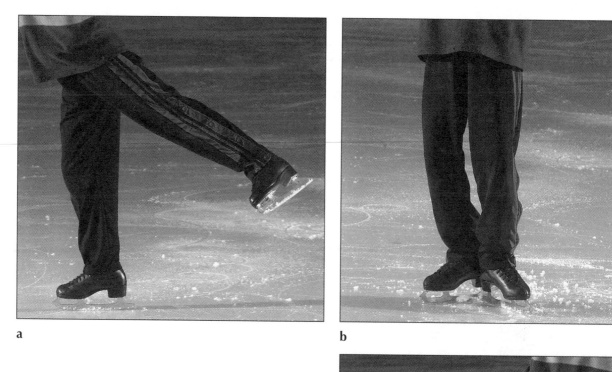

Figure 6.3   Inside open Mohawk: *(a)* Glide forward on an inside edge, *(b)* place the heel of the free foot against the instep of the skating foot, and *(c)* shift the weight to the new skating foot to reverse direction.

Inside Closed Mohawk

An inside closed Mohawk is executed just like an open Mohawk with one exception: when the free foot is placed on the ice to produce the back edge, the instep of the free foot is placed to the heel of the skating foot and the original skating foot (now the free foot) continues to move forward as the edge is finished. (See figure 6.4 a-c.) The difference between the open and closed Mohawk is, therefore, the placement of the new foot on the ice and the final position of the hip—open or closed.

a

b

c

Figure 6.4   Inside closed Mohawk: *(a)* Glide forward on an inside edge, *(b)* place the instep of the free foot to the heel of the skating foot, and *(c)* finish with a closed hip position.

Practice placing the free foot and stepping from the forward to the backward edge at the rink barrier before trying to execute the turn away from the barrier.

Variations on the Mohawk are often used in ice dancing, where there may be certain prescribed steps that must be incorporated into a dance and others that are listed as optional choices. In the Fiesta Tango, for example, the feet can immediately be placed together on the exit of the Mohawk. In the Swing Dance there is a prescribed extension of the free foot on the exit. Two such variations include the drop Mohawk and swing Mohawk, which are described later. These are exceptions to the normal interpretation.

Outside Open Mohawk

A right forward outside open Mohawk begins on the right foot, moving forward on an outside edge. It ends on the left back outside edge.

PREPARATION

The right forward outside Mohawk begins on a right forward outside edge on a well-bent knee with the left (free) foot behind (figure 6.5a), the right arm in front, and the left arm in back. The right hip leads into the turn.

TURN

The skating knee straightens slightly as the left heel is brought into the instep of the right foot (figure 6.5b). The shoulders rotate into the turn just as in a three. The left foot is placed on the ice toward the ball of the foot. Care must be taken not to step on the right blade. The weight shifts from the right (skating) foot to the left (new skating) foot as it steps down on the ice on a bent knee on the left back outside edge (figure 6.5c). The shoulders, which rotated into the turn on entry, tighten to a checked position on the exit to hold and maintain the back outside edge. The free foot is held back over the tracing on the final edge.

a

b

c

Figure 6.5   Outside open Mohawk: *(a)* Glide forward on an outside edge, *(b)* place the heel of the free foot against the instep of the skating foot, and *(c)* shift the weight to the new skating foot to reverse directions.

This process should be repeated beginning on the left foot to execute a left forward outside open Mohawk.

> Practice the outside open step at the rink barrier to become familiar with the action of the foot before trying it out on the ice. Repeat the step several times from right to left and then left to right. Once you move away from the barrier, practice a two-footed forward outside open Mohawk before trying to do the turn on one foot.

Outside Closed Mohawk

The outside closed Mohawk follows the same procedure as the open Mohawk except that when the free foot is placed on the ice to produce the back edge, the instep of the free foot is placed to the heel of the skating foot and the free foot continues forward on the finished edge. See figure 6.6 a-c.

a

b

c

Figure 6.6   Outside closed Mohawk: *(a)* Glide forward on an outside edge, *(b)* place the instep of the free foot to the heel of the skating foot, and *(c)* finish with a closed hip position.

Back Mohawk

A back Mohawk is a simple step from a back edge to the same edge going forward. There is no change of circle. If the circle or edge changes, the step becomes a Choctaw, which is discussed in the next segment. A back Mohawk is so natural that it is not even thought of as a Mohawk but rather as an automatic step from a back edge to a forward edge.

Drop Mohawk

Drop Mohawks are done in prescribed ice dances and in Moves in the Field tests. In a drop Mohawk the feet come together immediately following the turn, making three steps instead of two. Following the step down on the ice, the free foot is extended forward. A drop Mohawk is executed in the eight step Mohawk, which is an element in Moves in the Field.

Swing Mohawk

In a swing Mohawk the free foot swings past the skating foot before the foot is placed for the turn. In ice dancing both the man and the lady execute swing closed Mohawks in the Tango. Sometimes swing Mohawks are also incorporated into footwork sequences in skating routines.

Choctaws

A Choctaw is another variation in turning direction. A three turn rotates on one foot and a Mohawk on two feet; the Choctaw is similar to the Mohawk in that it changes direction and feet, but unlike the Mohawk it also changes edges.

Outside Choctaw

A right forward outside Choctaw begins on the right foot, moving forward on an outside edge. It ends on the left back inside edge. In ice dancing this turn is executed in the Quickstep and the Blues, as well as the Ravensburger Waltz, and the Tango Romantica.

PREPARATION

A right forward outside Choctaw starts on the right forward outside edge with the free foot behind and over the print (figure 6.7a). The right arm should be in front of the body and the left arm behind.

TURN

The left (free) foot is placed on the ice to the heel of the right (skating) foot on a back inside edge (figure 6.7b). As the right foot is picked up it moves forward and over the print (figure 6.7c). There is a slight pushing motion at the point of the turn. The body weight rocks to the ball of the foot on the outside edge and there is a twisting action in the hips as the feet and direction change. The right arm ends up leading and the left arm trailing.

a

b

c

Figure 6.7   Outside Choctaw: *(a)* Glide forward on an outside edge, *(b)* place the free foot to the heel of the skating foot, and *(c)* shift the weight to the inside edge of the new skating foot to change direction.

Both right and left foot Choctaws should be practiced, although the only Choctaw done on the right foot in dance is in the man's step on the Tango Romantica. If the Choctaw is done as a freestyle move, it is helpful to have the free foot swing forward to begin the momentum of the turn.

The best place to practice this turn is at the rink barrier. Develop a good feeling for the body and foot positions before trying the move out on the ice. Two-footed turns always help before trying one-footed turns.

Inside Choctaw

A left forward inside Choctaw begins on the left foot, moving forward on an inside edge. It finishes on the right back outside edge. This turn is executed in ice dancing in the Blues.

PREPARATION

A left forward inside Choctaw begins on the left forward inside edge with the free foot behind and over the print (figure 6.8a). The left arm should be in front of the body and the right arm behind.

TURN

The shoulders begin to rotate back into a checked position before the right foot is placed on the ice. The right (free) foot is placed on the ice to the heel of the left (skating) foot on a back outside edge. The left foot is picked up and lifted forward and over the print. The body weight rocks to the ball of the foot on the inside edge and the hips twist as the feet and direction change (figure 6.8b). At the finish the left arm leads and the right arm trails.

Both right and left foot Choctaws should be practiced.

a   b

Figure 6.8 Inside Choctaw: *(a)* Glide forward on an inside edge, place the free foot to the heel of the skating foot, and *(b)* shift the weight to the outside edge of the new skating foot.

Open Choctaw

In an open Choctaw the free foot is placed at the toe of the skating foot for the turn (figure 6.9), and after the turn the new free foot is behind the skating foot with the free hip checked back. An open Choctaw is executed in the Kilian in ice dancing.

Figure 6.9 In an open Choctaw the free foot is placed at the toe of the skating foot for the turn.

Figure 6.10 In a closed Choctaw the free foot is placed at the heel of the skating foot for the turn.

Junior Choctaw

In a junior Choctaw (a forward or backward wide open Choctaw) the foot is placed wide instead of close as in a standard open Choctaw.

Closed Choctaw

In a closed Choctaw the free foot is placed at the heel of the skating foot (figure 6.10), and the new free foot is extended forward after the turn with the free hip pressed forward. It is executed in the Blues and in the novice test Rocker Foxtrot.

Swing Choctaw

On a swing Choctaw the free foot swings past the skating foot before the foot is placed for the turn. Both the man and the lady execute swing closed Choctaws in the Quickstep.

Back Choctaw

This step, from a back edge to the opposite edge going forward, produces a change of circle. It can be from an inside to outside or outside to inside edge. If the circle or edge does not change, the step is a back Mohawk.

Brackets

A bracket is another one-footed turn. Like threes, brackets change edge and direction but not feet. The difference between a three and a bracket is that a three rotates into the circle and a bracket turns outside the circle (figure 6.11). The rotation on a bracket is exactly opposite of that of a three.

Figure 6.11 The tracing on the ice resulting from a bracket.

Forward Inside Bracket

A right forward inside bracket begins on the right foot, moving forward on an inside edge. It ends on the right back outside edge.

PREPARATION

A right forward inside bracket starts on the curve of a circle on a right forward inside edge. The left arm is forward, the right arm behind, and the left (free) foot in front. The head is looking forward toward the place where the bracket will be turned. It continues to look in the direction of travel throughout the entire turn.

TURN

As the turn approaches the body begins to rotate outside the circle in a clockwise direction. At the shoulder of the turn the upper body is tightly rotated with the left arm across in front of the body and the right arm pulling (**countering**) behind. The torso provides pressure against the arms. The skating knee is bent. During the turn the body weight, which began back of center on the forward edge going into the turn, rocks forward to just behind the bottom pick of the blade. At the same time the knee begins to straighten, helping the weight rock to the front of the blade. This shift allows the heel of the blade to lift and swing from a forward inside edge to a back outside edge. At the apex of the turn, as the blade is turning from front to back, the arms counter against the hips to control the checked position on the exit of the turn. The balance over the blade is now front of center, and the left arm is leading over the print while the right arm is trailing. The left (free) foot assists in the turn by lifting up slightly and then, at the exit of the turn, moves back to the heel of the right (skating) foot slightly to the inside of the circle.

Forward inside brackets should be practiced on both the right foot and the left foot.

Practice the bracket turn and the free foot action at the rink barrier and on two feet on a circle before executing a one-footed turn. The pattern resulting from a bracket on a circle is shown in figure 6.12.

Figure 6.12 Forward bracket on a circle.

Forward Outside Bracket

A right forward outside bracket begins on the right foot, moving forward on an outside edge. It finishes on the right back inside edge.

PREPARATION

To begin a right forward outside bracket, start on the curve of a circle on a right forward outside edge with the right arm forward, the left arm behind, and the left (free) foot placed to the heel of the right foot. The head should be looking forward and to the place where the bracket will be turned.

TURN

At the approach to the turn the body begins to rotate outside the circle in a counterclockwise direction. At the shoulder of the turn the upper body rotates tightly. The right arm crosses in front of the body and the left arm counters behind, with the torso providing pressure against the arms. The skating knee is bent. As the bracket is turned the body weight, which began back of center on the forward edge going into the turn, rocks forward to just behind the bottom pick of the blade, allowing the heel of the blade to lift and swing from a forward outside edge to a back inside edge. At the same time the knee straightens, helping the weight rock to the front of the blade. At the apex of the turn, as the blade is turning from front to back, the arms and shoulders counter against the hips to control the checked position on the exit of the turn. The balance over the blade is now front of center, and the right arm continues to lead over the print while the left arm trails. The left (free) leg assists in the turn by lifting up slightly, beginning with a bent knee and then straightening as it moves from the position behind the skating foot to a trailing position over the print on the exit. The head turns and looks back into the circle.

Both right and left forward outside brackets should be practiced.

Back Outside Bracket

A right back outside bracket begins on the right foot, moving backward on an outside edge. It ends on the right forward inside edge.

PREPARATION

The right back outside brackets start on the curve of a circle on a right back outside edge with the right arm leading, the left arm trailing, and the left (free) foot placed at the heel of the right (skating) foot. The head is looking to the place where the bracket will be turned and remains looking ahead after the turn.

TURN

On the approach the body begins to rotate outside the circle in a clockwise direction. The upper body rotates tightly at the shoulder of the turn, crossing the left arm in front of the body and countering the right arm behind. The torso provides pressure against the arms, and the skating knee is bent. During the turn the body weight, which began front of center on the back edge going into the turn, rocks back to just behind the center of the blade. This weight change allows the front of the blade to lift and change from a back outside edge to a forward inside edge. At the same time the knee straightens, assisting the weight as it rocks to the back of the blade. At the apex of the turn, as the blade is turning from back to front, the arms counter against the hips to control the checked position on the exit of the turn. The balance over the blade is now back of center, and the right arm is leading over the print while the left arm is trailing. The left (free) foot assists in the turn by lifting up slightly and then lowering to the back of the heel of the right (skating) foot at the exit.

Back outside brackets should be practiced on both feet.

Back Inside Bracket

A right back inside bracket begins on the right foot, moving backward on an inside edge. It finishes on a right forward outside edge.

PREPARATION

To begin a right back inside bracket, start on the curve of a circle on a right back inside edge with the left arm leading, the right arm trailing, and the left (free) foot in back of the skating foot. The head is looking forward and to the place where the bracket will be turned; it continues to look in the direction of travel throughout the entire turn.

TURN

The body begins to rotate outside the circle on the approach to the turn. At the shoulder of the turn the upper body rotates tightly. The right arm crosses in front of the body and the left arm continues to rotate behind, with the torso providing pressure against the arms. The skating knee is bent. During the turn the body weight, which began front of center on the back edge going into the turn, rocks back to just behind the center of the blade, allowing the front of the blade to lift and swing from a back inside edge to a forward outside edge. At the same time the knee straightens, helping the weight rock to the back of the blade. As the blade turns from back to front at the apex of the turn, the arms counter against the hips to control the checked position on the exit of the turn. The balance over the blade is now back of center. The left arm is leading over the print while the right arm is behind. The left (free) foot assists in the turn by lifting up slightly and then lowering to the back of the heel of the right (skating) foot at the exit of the turn.

Both right and left back inside brackets should be practiced.

Advanced Back Bracket

To create more depth in the bracket, a scissor action of the free foot is used to counter the turning action of the skating foot. As the skating foot moves back, the free foot swings forward. This action takes practice to develop coordination and timing.

Counters

A counter is similar to a bracket in that it turns against the natural rotation of the curve. A counter does not change edge or feet. It changes direction and travels from one circle to another. A counter is similar to a change of edge except that a turn in the center of the change faces into the direction of a new circle as shown in figure 6.13.

Figure 6.13 Counter on a circle.

Forward Inside Counter

A right forward inside counter begins on the right foot, going forward on an inside edge. It ends on a right back inside edge.

PREPARATION

To begin a right forward inside counter, start on a right forward inside edge. The left (free) foot is in front and over the print, the left arm is forward, and the right arm is in back. The head is looking forward to where the counter will be executed. The weight over the blade is back of center, and the skating knee is bent.

TURN

On the approach to the turn, the body begins to rotate outside the original circle. At the shoulder of the turn the upper body rotates tightly in a clockwise direction. The left arm is crossed in front of the body and the right arm is countering behind, with the torso providing pressure against the arms. As the counter is turned the body weight, which began back of center on the forward edge going into the turn, rocks forward to just behind the bottom pick of the blade. At the same time the knee straightens, helping the weight rock to the front of the blade without going to the toe pick. This shift allows the heel of the blade to lift and rotate through the turn without scraping as the direction changes from forward to backward without changing edge, and a new circle is introduced. At the apex of the turn, as the blade is turning from front to back, the arms counter against the hips to control the checked position on the exit of the turn. The balance over the blade is now front of center, and the left arm leads over the print while the right arm trails. The left (free) foot assists in the turn by scissoring from front to back and then returns past the skating foot, finishing in a trailing position over the print of the circle at the exit of the turn. The head continues to look ahead into the new circle in the direction of travel.

Practice both right and left forward inside counters.

Practice the turn and the scissor action at the rink barrier and on two feet on a circle before doing a one-footed counter.

Forward Outside Counter

A right forward outside counter begins on the right foot, going forward on an outside edge. It ends on a right back outside edge.

PREPARATION

To begin a right forward outside counter, start on a right forward outside edge. The left (free) foot is passed forward and over the print, the left arm is trailing, and the right arm is leading. The head is looking forward and to where the counter will be placed. The weight over the blade is back of center, and the skating knee is bent.

TURN

The body begins to rotate outside the original circle as the turn approaches and then, at the shoulder of the turn, the upper body rotates tightly counterclockwise. The right arm moves across in front of the body and the left arm counters behind, while the torso provides pressure against the arms. The body weight, which began back of center on the forward edge going into the turn, rocks forward during the turn to just behind the bottom pick of the blade, allowing the heel of the blade to lift and rotate through the turn without scraping. At the same time the knee straightens to help the weight rock to the front of the blade without going to the toe pick. The direction changes from forward to backward without changing edge as a new circle is begun. As the blade turns from front to back at the apex of the turn the arms counter against the hips to control the checked position on the exit. The balance over the blade is now front of center, and the right arm is leading over the print while the left arm is trailing. The left (free) foot assists in the turn by lifting and bending at the knee and scissoring from front to back. It then returns over the skating foot and over the print of the circle at the exit of the turn. The head continues to look ahead into the new circle in the direction of travel.

Forward outside counters should be practiced on both the right foot and the left.

Back Inside Counter

A right back inside counter starts on the right foot, moving backward on an inside edge. It finishes on a right forward inside edge.

PREPARATION

To begin a right back inside counter, start on a right back inside edge. The left (free) foot should be brought to the heel of the skating foot and carried over the print. The left arm is leading and the right arm is trailing. The head is looking ahead to where the counter will be placed. The weight over the blade is front of center, and the skating knee is bent.

TURN

As the turn is approached the body begins to rotate outside the circle. At the shoulder of the turn the upper body rotates tightly with the right arm across in front of the body and the left arm countering behind. The torso provides pressure against the arms. The skating knee is bent. As the counter is turned the body weight, which began front of center on the back edge going into the turn, rocks back to just behind the center of the blade, allowing the front of the blade to lift and swing from a backward to a forward direction on a new circle without changing edge. The knee simultaneously straightens to assist the weight in rocking to the back of the blade. At the apex of the turn, as the blade is turning from back to front, the arms counter against the hips to control the checked position on the exit. The balance over the blade is now back of center, and the left arm is leading over the print while the right arm is behind. The left (free) foot assists in the turn by lifting up slightly and then, with a scissor action, kicking into the new circle before moving back to the heel of the right (skating) foot at the exit of the turn.

Both right and left back inside counters should be practiced.

Back Outside Counter

A right back outside counter begins on the right foot, moving backward on an outside edge. It ends on a right forward outside edge.

PREPARATION

> To begin a right back outside counter, start on a right back outside edge. The left (free) foot is behind and over the print, the right arm is leading, and the left arm is trailing. The head is looking ahead to where the counter will be placed. The weight over the blade is front of center, and the skating knee is bent.

TURN

> On the approach to the turn the body begins to rotate inside the circle, while the blade is on an outside edge. The upper body rotates tightly at the shoulder of the turn. The left arm crosses in front of the body and the right arm counters behind, while the torso provides pressure against the arms. The skating knee is bent. The knee straightens and the body weight, which began front of center on the back edge going into the turn, rocks back to just behind the center of the blade during the turn. This weight change allows the front of the blade to lift and swing from a backward to a forward direction without changing edge as a new circle is begun. The arms counter against the hips at the apex of the turn, as the blade is turning from back to front, to control the checked position on the exit. The balance over the blade is now front of center. The right arm is leading over the print while the left arm is trailing. The left (free) foot lifts up slightly and then, in a scissor action, kicks into the original circle and back to the heel of the right (skating) foot at the exit of the turn.

> Back outside counters should be practiced on both feet.

Rockers

The rocker is similar to a three turn and, like a three turn, rotates inside the circle. A rocker does not change edge or feet but does change direction. It also travels from one circle to another. It is similar to a change of edge but has a turn in the center of the change, which faces into the direction of the original circle. (See figure 6.14.)

Forward Inside Rocker

A right forward inside rocker begins on the right foot, moving forward on an inside edge. It finishes on a right back inside edge.

Figure 6.14 Rocker on a circle.

PREPARATION

> To begin a right forward inside rocker, start on a right forward inside edge. The left (free) foot is in front and over the print, the right arm is forward, and the left arm is in back. The head is looking forward to where the rocker will be executed. The weight over the blade is back of center, and the skating knee is bent.

TURN

> The body begins to rotate into the circle as the turn approaches. At the shoulder of the turn the upper body rotates tightly. The right arm crosses in front of the body and the left arm rotates behind. The torso provides pressure against the arms. The body weight, which began back of center on the forward edge going into

the turn, rocks forward during the rocker to just behind the bottom pick of the blade. At the same time the knee straightens, helping the weight to rock to the front of the blade without going to the toe pick. This weight transfer allows the heel of the blade to lift and rotate through the turn without scraping the ice as the direction changes from forward to backward. There should be no change of edge as the new circle is introduced. At the apex of the turn, as the blade is turning from front to back, the arms rotate against the hips to control the checked position on the exit. After the turn the balance over the blade is front of center. The left arm leads over the print while the right arm trails. The left (free) foot assists in the turn by scissoring from front to back into the new circle and then returns over the skating foot and over the print of the new circle at the exit of the turn. The head turns to look into the new circle in the direction of travel.

Both right and left forward inside rockers should be practiced.

Practice the rocker and the free foot action at the rink barrier and on two feet on a circle before executing a one-footed turn. To practice the scissor action, face the barrier and hold on to it with both hands. Standing on one foot, let the skating foot move toward and away from the barrier as you swing the other foot in the opposite direction. Increase speed as your agility improves, and practice on both the right and left feet.

Forward Outside Rocker

A right forward outside rocker starts on the right foot, moving forward on an outside edge. It ends up on the right back outside edge.

PREPARATION

To begin a right forward outside rocker, start on a right forward outside edge with the left (free) foot in front and over the print, the left arm forward, and the right arm in back. The head should look forward to where the rocker will be executed. The weight over the blade is back of center, and the skating knee is bent.

TURN

On the approach to the turn the body begins to rotate into the circle. The upper body rotates tightly at the shoulder of the turn, with the left arm across in front of the body and the right arm rotated behind. The torso provides pressure against the arms. During the turn the knees straightens and the body weight, which began back of center on the forward edge going into the turn, rocks forward to just behind the bottom pick of the blade, which allows the heel of the blade to lift and rotate through the turn without scraping. A new circle is begun as the direction changes from forward to backward without changing edge. At the apex of the turn, as the blade is turning from front to back, the arms rotate against the hips to control the checked position on the exit. After the turn the balance over the blade is front of center, and the left arm leads over the print while the right arm trails. The left (free) foot scissors from front to back and then returns over the skating foot and over the print of the circle at the exit of the turn. The head looks to the outside of the new circle in the direction of travel.

Both right and left forward outside rockers should be practiced.

Back Inside Rocker

A right back inside rocker begins on the right foot, moving backward on an inside edge. It finishes on the right forward inside edge.

PREPARATION

A right back inside rocker starts on a right back inside edge. The left (free) foot is behind and over the print, the right arm is leading, and the left arm is trailing. The head is looking outside the circle to where the rocker will be placed. The weight over the blade is back of center, and the skating knee is bent.

TURN

The body begins to rotate outside the circle as the turn approaches. At the shoulder of the turn the upper body rotates tightly. The left arm moves across in front of the body and the right arm rotates behind, with the torso providing pressure against the arms. The body weight, which began front of center on the back edge going into the turn, now rocks to back of center on the blade. Simultaneously the knee straightens, assisting the weight as it rocks to the back of the blade without going to the heel. This weight transfer allows the toe of the blade to lift and rotate through the turn without scraping as the direction changes from backward to forward (without changing edge) and a new circle is begun. The arms rotate against the hips at the apex of the turn, as the blade is turning from back to front, to control the checked position on the exit. The balance over the blade after the turn is back of center. The right arm leads over the print and the left arm trails. The left (free) foot, which assists in the turn by scissoring from back to front, returns to the heel of the skating foot and over the print of the circle at the exit of the turn. The head continues to look ahead into the new circle in the direction of travel.

Both right and left back inside rockers should be practiced.

Back Outside Rocker

A right back outside rocker begins on the right foot, moving backward on an outside edge. It ends on a right forward outside edge.

PREPARATION

To begin a right back outside rocker, start on a right back outside edge. The left (free) foot is trailing and held over the print, the right arm is leading, and the left arm is trailing. The head begins by looking into the circle but rotates to the outside of the circle to where the rocker will be placed. The weight over the blade is front of center, and the skating knee is bent.

TURN

The body begins to rotate outside the circle at the quarter mark and continues as the turn approaches until, at the shoulder of the turn, the upper body is tightly rotated with the right arm across in front of the body and the left arm rotated behind. The torso provides pressure against the arms. During the turn the body weight, which began front of center on the back edge going into the turn, rocks to back of center on the blade to allow the toe of the blade to lift and rotate through the turn without scraping. The knee straightens simultaneously, helping the weight rock to the back of the blade without going to the heel. The direction changes from backward to forward on a new circle with no change of edge. As the blade turns from back to front at the apex of the turn, the arms rotate against the hips to control the checked position on the exit. The balance over the blade finishes back of center. The left arm leads over the print and the right arm trails. The left (free) foot scissors from back to front to assist the turn, then returns to the heel of the skating foot over the print of the circle at the exit of the turn. The head continues to look ahead into the new circle in the direction of travel.

Back outside rockers should be practiced on both the right and left feet.

Footwork

Footwork is a combination of turns and freestyle moves that, together, are the glue that holds a program together. There are three basic types of footwork—straight line, circular, and serpentine. These terms describe the pattern of the footwork.

In straight line, the steps and turns must lead from one end of the rink to the other, either commencing approximately at one corner of the ice surface and ending near the diagonally opposite corner, or following the long axis for the full length of the ice surface. In circular footwork the rule is that the moves must create a complete circle or oval utilizing the full width of the ice surface. Serpentine footwork begins at one end of the ice surface, progresses in at least two bold curves of not less than one half of the width of the ice surface, and ends at the opposite end of the rink. It is executed in an S or serpentine pattern. Key words in these descriptions are "bold," "at least," "full," "complete," "must," and "not less." These provisions must be followed or the judges will deduct marks.

Footwork also includes spiral sequences, which consist of spirals that commence at one end of the ice surface, progress in bold curves, and end at the opposite end of the rink; spirals that form a complete circle or oval, utilizing the full width of the ice surface; or a combination of the two.

In addition to the steps that are executed in the footwork, carriage, style, speed, flow, and quickness are elements that must also be demonstrated. Not only must the feet show depth and sureness of edges, but the arm positions and the turning of the head must also be developed in time with the music. Rhythm and timing are integral components of good footwork.

Good footwork changes rotational direction; incorporates highs and lows; uses a variety of complex turns; and is sure, quick, and smooth. Connecting steps include turns as well as spirals, lunges, half jumps, and creative movements—all in perfect timing to the music, adding character and drama to the program.

Footwork presents an opportunity for skaters to project personality. They can incorporate folk, ethnic, and character dances. They can also reflect humor, as Olympic champion Scott Hamilton and Canadian champion Kurt Browning have marvelously demonstrated.

Master the Move

Scott Hamilton's Innovative Footwork

The creativity, expression, and precision of Hamilton's footwork are what make his programs stand out.

No one is more loved in today's skating world than Scott Hamilton. He captivates audiences with his creativity and expression while impressing judges with the intricacy and precision of his moves. His footwork is legendary. His combinations of turns and freestyle moves are original and, oftentimes, humorous.

At a time when footwork was not appreciated as much as it is today, Hamilton understood the value of exciting and innovative connecting steps. He was one of the first skaters to not just skate to the music but also to project his personality through his interpretive footwork.

Steps can set the tone of the program as proven by one of the best in the world. Creativity counts and so do strong edges, movements in both directions, and surprise elements. Edges should be clean, quick, and sure. Hamilton is always developing a new angle or approach, and you can do the same by using music, creative steps and turns, and expressive arm and head movements to personalize your program. Character and expression in footwork separates those who merely do the steps from those who perform well-choreographed programs.

Deftness and flexibility are assets that enhance good footwork. The new Moves in the Field format has been developed to add quickness, power, quality of edge, speed, and extension to connecting steps in a program. While turns executed in Moves in the Field differ from turns done in compulsory figures or dance, each discipline has an important emphasis that helps to strengthen and train a good skater. As mentioned earlier, Moves in the Field have adapted turns from dance and figures that were precisely skated and judged. In figures it was mandatory that the judges stand on the ice while the figure was being performed. Upon its completion they would walk around, over, and across the figure measuring its size, quality, and precision. Because Moves in the Field are done as a freestyle element and are executed with great speed, the judges are seated at the side of the rink and the perfection of the turn is not as important, nor can it be measured as easily.

Summary

Ice dancing and figures have been the basis for all turns. Since the elimination of figures several years ago, the only remaining discipline for perfecting steps and turns is dance. The newly created Moves in the Field incorporates turns, but it is not a discipline in itself. With the increased speed and power used by skaters today, turns as they were known in the 20th century will be lost to future generations. Preserving this technique is important so that a greater understanding of balance, rock, edge, timing, and body and blade placement are described in detail for future reference and understanding.

Just as important as preserving technique in turns, however, is adding originality and character to a program through footwork. The complexity and intricacy of footwork, enhanced by strong edges, can make an ordinary program extraordinary. It is not unlike a fresh interpretation of a piece of music or the personalization of artwork. Each skater can, and must, create an individual expression in footwork. This individuality becomes a part of the theme of the program as well as an expression of the skater's own character. It is unlike prescribed moves such as jumps or spins, where the takeoff edge, body position, and landing are alike for every skater. To complete all the required elements in a program and to have innovative and creative footwork separates the ordinary from the extraordinary.

chapter 7
Spins

A well-balanced freestyle program contains three primary elements: jumps, spins, and footwork. Spins do not get the same credit as jumps, but the skating world is beginning to take notice and give credit for quality spins. There are four basic spins: the upright, the camel, the sit, and the layback. In recent years innovative positions have created highly interesting and unusually artistic spins such as the Biellmann.

A spin combines two forces: centripetal and centrifugal. Skaters feel centripetal forces when they draw their arms and legs in tightly toward the center of their bodies. Centrifugal force is just the opposite. It's the force that pushes the arms and legs away. It's the perfect balance between these two forces and the artistry of the skater's position that creates an exciting and beautiful spin.

Spinning Fundamentals

Spins can be classified into two general categories: flat spins and toe spins. This terminology refers to the part of the blade the skater is on when spinning. Flat spins are executed just behind the toe pick on the front part of the blade and can include camel spins and sit spins, as well as any of their variations. Toe spins are executed farther to the front of the blade, catching the first toe pick. These spins and their variations include one-footed, scratch, and layback spins.

The object of every spin, whether it's a flat spin or a toe spin, is to be fast, controlled, centered, and in a good position. A good spin rotates over one spot and does not **travel** across the ice. In a jump the approach is progressive, moving across the ice from takeoff to landing. The approach to a spin is exactly opposite in that the skater moves forward in one direction and then reverses to the other. Despite this difference, spinning techniques are still the basis for all jumps. For example, the air position in a multi-rotational jump is a tightly closed back scratch spin.

It is extremely important to determine which direction a skater will jump and spin—clockwise or counterclockwise. It is also critical that the skater jump and spin in the same direction. Methods for determining which direction is best for a skater are discussed at the beginning of chapter 8.

Before moving on to the technique for individual spins, it's important to understand some of the general principles that apply to all spins. The following information on entering and exiting the spin, centering, positioning the arms, and increasing the speed of rotation holds true for all types of spins.

Spin Entry

Spins typically begin from back crossovers. The right back inside edge of the last crossover is held (figure 7.1a), and the left leg, keeping a well-bent knee, steps into the circle formed by the curve of that edge (figure 7.1b). A small, tight three turn occurs at the entry into every spin. The skating knee remains bent until after the three "hooks" the spin, catching the first tooth of the toe pick on a back inside edge. After one turn has been completed the knee straightens, keeping the balance forward on the blade.

It's important to step *into* the circle off the inside edge, rather than out of the circle. The difference is shown in figure 7.2.

This chapter was written by Carole Shulman and reviewed by Janet Champion. Champion began her teaching career in 1968 and has been a spin coach to World and Olympic champions. She holds a master rating in figures, freestyle, group skating, and Moves in the Field.

a   b

Figure 7.1   Spin entry: *(a)* The right back inside edge is held, then *(b)* the left foot steps into the circle.

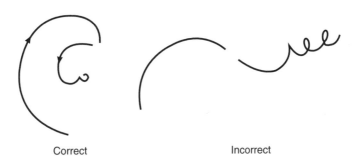

Correct   Incorrect

Figure 7.2   During the entry, step *into* the circle off the inside edge, not out of the circle.

An alternate (but less commonly used) entry begins the spin from a right forward inside three, stepping from the back outside edge onto a left forward outside edge to begin the rotation into the spin. This method is more difficult for the beginning skater.

Centering Spins

The most important part of a spin is the centering. A good spin is centered, which means that the body is in perfect balance over the blade, the shoulders and hips are square, the back is erect, and the spin remains in one spot. A spin requires the conversion of forward momentum into rotational force. To achieve this, the entry edge of a spin must be a curve whose diameter diminishes as it approaches the three.

The print on the ice will leave small concentric circles placed closely beside the entry three. A traveling spin is considered a fault and will leave a print that looks like tiny looping circles spread out across the ice. See figure 7.3. The more the spin travels, the wider the spread between the loops.

Either of two common mistakes can cause a spin to travel: a shallow entry edge or an entry edge that does not progressively diminish in diameter as it approaches the three. Allowing the free leg to swing around before the point of the turn causes the spin to begin before the entry edge has diminished sufficiently.

Entry edge techniques that assist in centering spins are maintaining the body weight over the skating side and leaning into the entry edge circle, which helps to make the edge a diminishing curve. It is also helpful to skate a strong, deep entry edge, keeping the free leg stretched and held firmly behind the body until the point of the three. The skating knee should stay bent until at least one full turn is completed.

Keeping the following points in mind will help keep a spin centered:

- The shoulders should be level and down.
- The hips should be level and square.
- The free leg should be controlled and extended.
- After the spin is hooked the arms and free leg should reach their final position.
- The skating foot should make smooth, even, little circles.
- Centrifugal force will pull out on the arms and the free leg once they are relaxed.

Correct   Incorrect

Figure 7.3   The spin must be skated in circles, not loops.

Arm Positions

There are two schools of thought on the position of the arms when entering a spin. Knowing both methods allows a skater to accommodate errors in a spin by using one position over the other. The most common method is to bring the left arm across in front of the body with the right arm behind in a counter-rotated position. The lead (skating) arm remains forward over the print as the body steps into the spin. As the three is hooked, the arm rotates into its final position. It is important to remain on an even plane so as to not drop the shoulders, which would cause an imbalance at the beginning of the spin. The advantage of this method is that the arm stays set on the entry and generates momentum as you step into the spin on the entry edge. If the arm is allowed to swing across the body, the spin may travel.

The second method is to rotate the arms before stepping into the spin, while still on the back inside edge. The right arm leads across in front of the body and over the print, pulling the left arm strongly behind, so that the step into the spin is cleared with the shoulders already rotated and the hips square to the print. This method reduces the chance of the skater's balance being offset, as can occur if the arms are allowed to swing across the body, but generating the initial momentum going into the spin is more difficult with this technique.

Speed of Rotation

Beyond centering and controlling spins, increasing and maintaining speed, or velocity, is the most important element of a good spin. *Angular velocity* implies rotation.

Aerodynamically, the more streamlined the body, the greater the opportunity to increase speed. Just as an automotive designer incorporates sleek lines into a race car, skaters must also design their spinning positions to allow for the least wind resistance. A scratch spin will obviously have greater speed than a camel spin.

As stated earlier, centripetal and centrifugal forces play a great role in spinning. Centripetal force tends to make rotating bodies move toward the center of rotation. Centrifugal force makes rotating bodies move away from the center of rotation. Overcoming the centrifugal force by pulling the arms in toward the body is what makes a spin go faster. When a skater draws the arms and legs tightly toward the center of the body, the speed increases. The primary motions that skaters use to increase speed are *in* and *down*.

Once a spin position is struck, the balance over the blade must be maintained to continue the momentum. Any movement back and forth on the blade will immediately diminish the speed. The only way to regain control is to open up the spin position and begin to pull in once again.

Newton's third law of gravity applies to the skater: for every action there is an equal and opposite reaction. To maintain speed and continue rotation there must be a lifting and stretching opposed by a pulling and tightening. The more speed a skater generates at the beginning of the spin, the longer the spin will be held, provided that balance can be maintained. Like a top, a skater who loses balance on a fast spin literally flies out of control.

There are three primary elements that must be followed to increase angular velocity:

1. The arms must pull toward the rotational **axis**.
2. The hips must be kept over the spinning foot.
3. The head must be kept erect (in an upright spin).

Spins have a required number of rotations that must be completed in testing or competition. If the requirement is not met, deductions will be made. Both balance and speed are necessary to perform a good spin.

A good spin also requires the right focus, which combats the dizziness that many beginning skaters experience. NASA has done a number of tests using figure skaters to help understand and control the effects of dizziness. Scientists discovered that the technique perfected by an accomplished skater is to focus not on objects as they spin past but on the space between the skater and the object. With practice and increased skill, dizziness significantly diminishes.

Exit

A spin is exited by pushing off onto a right back outside edge, the same as for a right back outside push off. Normally all spins finish in the same final position as jumps, with the body erect, the free foot extended, the skating knee bent, the head up, and the arms out to the side .

Upright Spins

Upright spins are those that are performed with the body positioned upright over the skating foot. These are the basic spins on which all the others are formed. The principles of a good spin begin here and apply to all categories. Often, when problems occur in more advanced spins, it is wise to go back to the basic uprights and correct the errors that are usually found at this level. Nothing can replace a solid foundation.

All descriptions in this chapter are based on a rotation to the left, or counterclockwise. For a rotation to the right, reverse the description.

Figure 7.4   Two-footed spin.

Two-Footed Spin

Because a two-footed spin is the first spin a skater learns, the emphasis should be placed not on the entry or exit but solely on the mechanics of the spin itself. The spin is performed on two feet with the body erect, the head up, and the arms pulled in across the chest.

PREPARATION

The two-footed spin starts on two feet about shoulder-width apart on the flat of the blades. The knees are bent and both arms are over to the right side.

SPIN

The arms and shoulders swing across to the left side as the knees are straightened. For a beginning skater the toes should be slightly turned in to form a triangular platform on which to spin. A more advanced skater will begin to feel the weight of the left foot toward the ball on a left back inside edge and the weight of the right foot toward the heel on a right forward inside edge. The body should follow the arms until the hips and shoulders are square. Once the body is in a balanced position the hands pull together in front of the body, and then the arms are drawn in, keeping the elbows up and the body square (figure 7.4).

One-Footed Spin

This spin is performed on the right foot with the left foot resting beside the knee of the skating leg. This is a solid, introductory spin.

PREPARATION

Begin from the left back inside edge by keeping the right (free) leg extended behind the body in line with the left (skating) foot. Then, with the right knee well bent and the shoulders level, the free leg steps into the circle on a strongly curving right forward outside edge. The body weight should be aligned over the skating hip.

SPIN

The left leg moves from back to front starting low to the ice and moving from an extended position in the back to a stretched position in front of the body at about the height of the skating hip. As the free leg swings around, the skating knee should straighten. A three turn on the right (skating) foot hooks the spin with the balance forward on the blade, catching the first tooth of the toe pick on a back inside edge. The arms should be out to the side. The free foot is brought straight in toward the body so that it rests beside the skating knee. As the free foot is drawn in, the arms are also drawn in toward the body to increase momentum. See figure 7.5.

EXIT

The free foot slowly lowers by sliding down the skating leg until the toe is resting beside the skating boot, and then the left foot is placed on the ice and pushes off onto a left back outside edge. The final position is held, demonstrating balance and control.

Figure 7.5 One-footed spin.

To understand the feeling of balance, introduce the one-footed spin by doing a two-footed spin and then lifting one foot off the ice, bending the knee of the free leg and placing the free foot beside the skating knee. It is best to try this when you're not spinning too fast. Keep the arms out to the side for balance.

Forward Open Spin

Before going farther, it's important for you to clarify the difference between forward and backward spins. The forward spin is a misnomer because the actual spin begins on the back inside edge. All back spins are defined by spinning on the back outside edge of the opposite foot. When rotating counterclockwise a forward spin is executed on the left foot and a back spin is executed on the right foot.

The forward open spin is exactly like the one-footed spin except that the free foot is held out to the side and not pulled in to the body.

PREPARATION

The setup begins from back crossovers. The last right back inside edge should be held with the left (free) leg extended behind the body in line with the right (skating) foot. Then the free foot steps into the circle on a strongly curving left forward outside edge, with the left knee well bent and the shoulders level. The body weight should be aligned over the skating hip.

SPIN

The right leg moves from back to side starting low to the ice and moving from an extended position in the back to a stretched position out to the side. The skating knee then straightens and the three turn hooks the spin with the balance forward on the blade, catching the first tooth of the toe pick on a back inside edge. The arms also remain out to the side in an open position. (See figure 7.6.)

EXIT

The right (free) leg lowers to the toe of the left (spinning) foot. Then the right foot steps down onto the ice, pushing off onto a right back outside edge. Holding the finish position demonstrates balance and control.

Figure 7.6   Forward open spin.

This spin is an exercise in itself, teaching balance and control. It is also used as a preparation for back spins or as a variation on the exit of other spins.

Back Open Spin

The back open spin is done on a right back outside edge. It exactly mirrors the forward open spin.

PREPARATION

Begin from back crossovers by holding the last right back inside edge, keeping the left (free) leg extended behind the body in line with the right (skating) foot. Then the left foot steps into the circle on a strongly curving left forward outside edge, with the left knee well bent and the shoulders level. The body weight should be aligned over the skating hip. The open spin position is held until balance is secure. Then the right (free) foot moves across in front of the left foot, and the left foot pushes off onto the toe of the right foot on a right back outside edge.

A second, more advanced entry method is to turn a right forward inside three, keeping the left (free) foot behind the right (skating) foot. When the three is completed, instead of the foot turning in toward the body, the body turns in toward the foot. This technique provides better balance and control.

SPIN

The right leg moves to a stretched position out to the side (figure 7.7). The arms also remain out to the side in an open position. The back open spin position should be held until balance and control are secure. The body weight is balanced just behind the toe of the right (skating) foot on a right back outside edge.

EXIT

The left (free) foot lowers and comes beside the toe of the right (spinning) foot. It pulls back to the toe of the right foot to slow the spin and then steps forward onto the left outside edge. The edge is held with the free foot extended behind the body over the print and the arms held out to the sides.

This spin is another exercise that helps develop balance and control. It is also used as preparation for learning the back scratch spin.

Figure 7.7 Back open spin.

Forward Scratch Spin

The forward scratch spin is like the one-footed spin, except that after one or more turns, the free foot crosses over the skating foot and rests to the outside of the ankle of the skating boot. This aerodynamic position, along with the inertia of the arms pulling in toward the body, creates a very fast spin that is commonly used to finish all other spins.

PREPARATION

The setup begins from back crossovers. The last right back inside edge should be held with the left (free) leg extended behind the body in line with the right (skating) foot. Then the free foot steps into the circle on a strongly curving left forward outside edge, with the left knee well bent and the shoulders level. The body weight should be aligned over the skating hip.

Figure 7.8   Forward scratch spin.

SPIN

The right leg moves from back to front starting low to the ice and moving from an extended position in the back to a stretched position in the front at about the height of the skating hip. As the free leg swings around, the skating knee straightens. The three turn hooks the spin with the balance forward on the blade, catching the first tooth of the toe pick on a back inside edge. The arms should be out to the side. The free foot is brought straight in toward the body so that it rests to the outside just above the skating knee, keeping the free leg knee turned out, or open.

As the free foot is drawn in, the arms come together in a circle in front of the body as though they were holding a very large pumpkin. The elbows must be kept up. The right (free) foot slowly lowers by sliding down the outside of the left (skating) leg, pressing the right heel down and lifting the right toe, until the right foot rests beside the left foot with the ankles crossed. The right heel continues to press down and the toe continues to point upward. As the foot pushes down, the hands simultaneously clasp together in the center front of the body and pull tightly in toward the body by bending at the elbows, then press down with the palms of the hands until the elbows are nearly straight. (See figure 7.8.) This movement increases momentum by creating the least resistance and therefore the greatest speed.

EXIT

The free leg lifts slightly to uncross at the ankle and then steps down on the right foot onto the ice, pushing off onto a right back outside edge. The finish position is held to demonstrate balance and control.

Another variation is to lift the arms up over the head instead of pushing them down. This is called a statue spin.

At the rink barrier, practice the crossed ankle position and the lifting of the free foot for the back push off. Develop increased strength in the arms through supervised off-ice conditioning and free weights as described in chapter 3.

Back Scratch Spin

The back scratch spin is executed on the right foot on a back outside edge. It is the opposite foot and edge from those used on a forward scratch spin.

PREPARATION

The back scratch spin can be entered using either of the entry methods described for the back open spin. The first of these methods can be shortened to a left forward outside three, pushing off onto a right back outside edge into the back spin position. If the second method is used, the curve of the back outside skating edge should tighten when the three is completed to begin the back spin. A third entry is from a right back inside pivot with the right toe in the ice, shifting the body weight completely over to the right back outside edge to begin the back spin.

SPIN

The back open spin position should be held until balance and control are secure. The arms should be out to the side. The free leg begins out to the side, but then the body turns in the direction of the foot while the foot remains in place, so that the foot is in front of the body. This placement provides better balance and control. After several rotations the free foot moves straight in toward the body so that it rests to the outside just above the skating knee, keeping the free leg knee turned out, or open. The weight of the body must be over the skating foot so that the toe pick is dragged backward in a small circle when spinning and not pushed forward.

Figure 7.9 Back scratch spin.

As the left (free) foot is drawn in, the arms come together in a circle in front of the body as though they were holding a very large pumpkin. The elbows must be kept up. The left foot slowly lowers by sliding down the outside of the skating leg while pressing down with the heel and lifting the toe. The left foot should rest beside the right (skating) foot, crossed at the ankle and continuing to press the heel down and point the toe up (figure 7.9). At the same time as the left foot is pushing down, the hands clasp together in the center front of the body and pull tightly in toward the body by bending at the elbows, then press down with the palms of the hands until the elbows are nearly straight. This movement increases momentum by creating the least resistance and therefore the greatest speed.

EXIT

Before the back scratch spin is exited, the left (free) foot, which is crossed at the right (skating) ankle, lifts up and over the skating foot, and the free leg snaps back in an extended position, remaining on the right back outside edge. This move is begun by pressing the toe pick of the skating foot forward to stop the rotation of the spin. The knee of the free leg must be well bent as the free foot is uncrossing.

At the same time the arms should be raised to a center front position with the hands continuing to stay together. When the free leg snaps back, the arms should also break out to the exit and finish position.

Use the exit of the back scratch spin as an exercise to practice learning how to stop rotation in jumps and prepare for the landing. Do a slow back spin, lifting the free leg and passing it quickly by the skating leg to simulate a jump landing, or stand at the rink barrier and practice the crossed ankle position and the release by lifting and snapping the free leg back. Increase the speed and timing by repeating this exercise over and over.

Figure 7.10   Position of the legs in the cross foot spin.

Cross Foot Spin

A cross foot spin is performed on two feet with the left foot crossed in front of the right, the toes pointed toward each other, and the heels apart (figure 7.10). There are three types of cross foot spins: the European, the American, and the two-footed, all of which are described in the following paragraphs.

PREPARATION

The cross foot spin is commonly begun from a two-footed spin or a forward or backward open spin, depending on which type of cross foot is being executed.

SPIN

The European cross foot spin begins with a left forward open spin, and then the right foot drops behind, passing over and behind the left heel with no hesitation. The spin must be performed on the right back outside edge, and the weight must shift to the outside of the left foot to change the pivotal axis and remain perfectly centered.

The American cross foot spin begins with a right back open spin, and then the left foot is placed on the ice in front of and beside the right foot in a toe-to-toe position.

The two-footed cross foot spin begins with the feet slightly wider apart then usual, and then the feet turn counterclockwise, twisting the right foot behind the left.

EXIT

On the exit of all types of cross foot spins, the left foot lifts up and over the right foot, and then the left (free) leg snaps back in an extended position, remaining on the right back outside edge.

Sit Spins

The second category of spins are sit spins. These spins are adapted from the shoot-the-duck position learned in the freestyle moves. Muscular strength is needed to control the sit position and, more importantly, to rise up from the sit spin. Before trying sit spins, it's important to master the shoot-the-duck, which helps develop the strength and balance needed for sit spins.

Forward Sit Spin

The basic sit spin is a forward shoot-the-duck executed in a spin.

PREPARATION

The forward sit spin begins from back crossovers. The last right back inside edge is held with the left (free) leg extended behind the body in line with the right (skating) foot. Then the left foot steps into the circle on a strongly curving left forward outside edge, with the knee well bent and the shoulders level. The body weight should be aligned over the skating hip. The skating knee continues into a deeper knee bend from back to front as the three turn hooks the spin with the balance forward on the blade, catching the first tooth of the toe pick on a back inside edge.

SPIN

As the right (free) leg swings around from back to front, the left (skating) knee should bend fully into the sit spin position. The arms should begin out to the side and then be brought forward, reaching out to the ankle of the free foot (figure 7.11). The free foot remains straight out in front in a position that is aligned in a straight line from the hip to the toe, parallel to the ice and level with the bent skating knee. The foot is turned out, and the back is straight but bent forward in about a 60-degree angle to the free leg.

Figure 7.11   Forward sit spin.

EXIT

A sit spin is exited by leaning slightly forward while simultaneously bringing the (right) free leg around in a circular motion and rising up on the left (skating) knee. The phrase "climb the lighthouse stairs" is an apt description of the rising action coming out of a sit spin. The free leg does not actually move. Instead, think about standing in the basement of a lighthouse and climbing the circular stairs to the top. Rising from a sit spin to an upright position creates the same sensation. When the body is fully erect the right foot will be in front and the left knee nearly straight. The spin pulls in and finishes exactly the same as a forward scratch spin.

The most important exercise to help you learn the sit spin is to develop the muscles necessary to lower and rise on one leg. You can develop this increased strength by doing supervised off-ice conditioning that includes squats and lunges or by practicing the bending and rising position at the rink barrier with the free leg in front of the body, being careful to keep the weight forward. This exercise is similar to the one learned for the lunge and the shoot-the-duck. Repeat it no more than five times on each foot (one for forward and one for back sit spins). When first doing this exercise, be careful not to overdo the repetitions as doing so may result in muscle strain.

Back Sit Spin

The back sit is similar to the forward sit except that it is done on the opposite foot and is entered either on a back outside edge or from a right forward inside three.

PREPARATION

Beginning from a forward open spin position, the right (free) foot moves across in front of the left foot. The left foot pushes off onto first the toe and then the ball of the right foot on a right back outside edge before the body lowers into the back sit position.

A second, more advanced entry method is to turn a right forward inside three, keeping the left (free) foot behind the right (skating) foot. When the three is completed, the body turns in toward the foot (the foot does not turn toward the body) and then lowers into a back sit position.

SPIN

The right (skating) knee should bend fully into the sit spin position and be balanced over the ball of the foot, not the toe pick. The arms should begin out to the side and then be brought forward, reaching out to the ankle of the left (free) foot. The left foot remains straight out in front of the body in a position that is ideally aligned in a straight line from the hip to the toe, parallel to the ice and level with the bent right knee. The left foot is turned out, and the back is straight but bent forward in about a 60-degree angle to the free leg.

EXIT

A back sit spin is exited by leaning slightly forward while at the same time keeping the left (free) leg in front to rise up on the right (skating) knee. When the body is fully erect the left foot will be in front of the body and the right knee nearly straight. The arms and free leg pull in and the spin finishes exactly the same as a back scratch spin.

Camel Spins

Camel spins make up the third category of spins. They are adapted from the spiral and in recent years have been varied by grasping the free leg and pulling it into a multitude of innovative and contorted positions.

Forward Camel

The basic camel spin is the forward camel, from which many variations have sprung.

PREPARATION

The setup begins from back crossovers. The last left back inside edge should be held with the right (free) leg extended behind the body in line with the left (skating) foot. Then the free foot steps into the circle on a strongly curving right forward outside edge, with the right knee well bent and the shoulders level. The body weight should be aligned over the skating hip. The skating knee continues into a deeper bend as the body leans forward in a spiral, or *arabesque*, position.

SPIN

As in all other spins, the three hooks the spin and the skating knee straightens with the balance forward on the blade, catching the first tooth of the toe pick. Keep the body weight on the ball of the foot on a back inside edge rather than on the toe pick. The spiral or camel position is held firmly by arching the back, stretching out the arms, holding the head up, and extending the neck (figure 7.12). When the spin is first being learned the arms should be held out to the side, but once the spin has

Figure 7.12   Forward camel spin.

been mastered arm variations can add interest. The right arm may reach forward and the left arm back, for example, or both hands may be locked behind the back.

An advanced variation of the camel spin is a forward outside camel, which is executed by shifting the weight farther to the back of the blade and spinning on a forward outside edge. The left hip and toe lift, and the weight shifts to the back of the blade.

EXIT

The left (free) leg lowers, and the body lifts to a vertical position while still spinning over the right foot. The free leg swings around to the front of the body. The arms pull in and finish exactly as in a forward scratch spin.

Catch Foot Camel

One variation of the forward camel is the catch foot camel, shown in figure 7.13. From the camel spin position the right hand reaches back to catch the right blade. The right leg will be bent. The preparation, spin, and exit phases are the same as for a forward camel.

Figure 7.13   Catch foot camel.

Curly Camel

Another variation is the curly camel, named by British coach Joan Ogilvie. From the camel spin position the left hand reaches back to catch the right blade (figure 7.14). The right leg will be bent, but the thigh remains parallel to the ice. Follow the same preparation, spin, and exit phases as for a forward camel.

Figure 7.14   Curly camel.

Back Camel

The back camel spin is similar to the forward camel, but it is done on the other foot on a back outside edge.

PREPARATION

Beginning from a forward open spin position, the right (free) foot moves across in front of the left foot and the left foot pushes off onto the toe of the right foot on a right back outside edge as the body leans forward in a spiral, or arabesque, position. This change from a front spin to a back spin is similar to the transition used in the back scratch spin, but the torso is bent forward during the change.

A second, more advanced entry method, is to turn a right forward inside three, keeping the left (free) foot behind the right (skating) foot. As the three is being completed, the left foot should be lifted from the ice in a spiraling counterclockwise rotation into the back camel position.

SPIN

To help control the back spin, the right arm pulls slightly toward the left free foot, creating tension and increased momentum. The skating knee should straighten, and the balance on the back camel should be toward the front of the blade on the right back outside edge. The arms should begin out to the side and change to more creative positions only after the back camel is mastered.

EXIT

On the exit from a back camel spin, the left (free) leg lowers and the body lifts to a vertical position while still spinning over the right foot. The body turns in toward the foot, then pulls in and finishes exactly as in a back scratch spin.

Off-ice stretching can improve camel spins and their variations. Place the free leg on a ballet barre, facing either toward the barre or away from it. Stretch out the muscles of both the elevated leg and the standing leg. Remember to lift the ribcage up and stretch the upper body before leaning forward. Always stretch out both legs to achieve a bilateral balance between the elevated and the standing leg.

Layback Spins

This section covers the layback spin and one of its variations, the Biellmann.

Layback

The layback is one of the most beautiful of all spins. Ladies perform it more frequently than men, although a few men have perfected lovely laybacks. The standard layback is executed on one foot while the body bends straight back from the waist and the arms are placed overhead in a graceful position. Side laybacks are an alternative to the standard layback and are frequently done because they are easier to perform.

PREPARATION

The setup for the layback is exactly the same as for a forward scratch spin except that the free foot begins in front and then is placed behind the skater.

SPIN

From the upright spin position the upper body turns away from the right (free) leg until it is positioned behind the left (skating) leg in an open, turned-out position. This is similar to the *attitude* position in ballet, but the thigh is not placed as high. The ideal placement of the free foot is directly behind the skating foot with the knee of the free leg at the same height or slightly higher than the free foot.

As the layback position begins from the hips and moves up the body to the head, the hips must first move slightly forward of the skating foot and then continue to bend back in a rolling action, so that the arch is felt at the waist and through the spine one vertebra at a time until the neck and head are also inclined backward. As the body leans back, the skating hips move forward to provide a counterbalance to the arch of the back (figure 7.15). Arm positions are optional. Both arms may be brought overhead, one may be held up and the other down, or both may be crossed in front of the chest. Creative variations in arm positions are encouraged and rewarded by the judges.

Figure 7.15   Layback spin.

EXIT

The body lifts slowly upright, reversing the entry procedure. Starting with the head and neck, each vertebra from top to bottom lifts until the body returns to a fully upright position. The right (free) leg is brought around to the front, and the spin finishes in a forward scratch spin, the same as for all other spins.

Practice backbends on the floor to increase flexibility. Hold onto the rink barrier and feel the layback position. Explore creative arm positions.

Biellmann

This spin is named after its creator, Swiss champion Denise Biellmann. An athletic variation and cross between the layback spin and the catch foot camel, it requires great flexibility: the skater must reach back for the blade of the free foot and pull the free leg overhead in a nearly split position while remaining upright over the skating foot.

PREPARATION

The setup for the Biellmann is exactly the same as for a forward scratch spin. It begins from back crossovers. The last right back inside edge should be held with the left (free) leg extended behind the body in line with the right (skating) foot.

Then the free leg steps into the circle on a strongly curving left forward outside edge, with the left knee well bent and the shoulders level. The body weight should be aligned over the skating hip.

SPIN

From the forward open spin position, the knee of the right (free) foot bends and the right hand reaches back for the blade of the free foot. With the palm facing upward the hand pulls the free foot up behind the head, and then the other hand grabs the blade so that both hands are on the blade. (One variation is to move the free leg to the front or side of the body instead of pulling it up from behind.) The foot continues to be lifted into the air above the head as both elbows extend and the head lies back to achieve maximum stretch (figure 7.16). The body is balanced forward on the blade, much the same as for a layback spin.

EXIT

The blade is released and the body returns to an upright position. The spin pulls in and finishes exactly the same as a forward scratch spin.

Figure 7.16 Biellmann spin.

Flexibility is key. Make sure you have a solid layback and have mastered the exercises suggested for the layback spin. Use the spin itself as an exercise to stretch out the muscles. Practice off the ice before attempting the Biellmann spin, making sure your body is fully warmed up before trying it on the ice.

Flying Spins

Flying spins combine jumps and spins. Each forward and back spin should be mastered and consistent before flying spins are undertaken. A good foundation in jumping basics is also required.

Flying Camel

A flying camel takes off from a left forward outside edge, jumping into the air with the body ideally parallel to the ice and then landing in a back camel spin. A 45-degree torso angle is also acceptable.

PREPARATION

The setup for the flying camel is the same as for the camel spin. The setup begins from back crossovers. The last right back inside edge should be held with the left (free) leg extended behind the body in line with the right (skating) foot. Then the free leg steps into the circle on a strongly curving left forward outside edge, with the left knee well bent and the shoulders level. The body weight should be aligned over the skating hip. The skating knee continues into a deeper knee bend as the body leans forward in a spiral, or arabesque, position. The right arm is trailing and the left arm is leading. An alternate method is to begin from a right forward inside three, stepping forward on a left outside edge as the body leans forward in a spiral position.

TAKEOFF

As the left forward outside edge is struck, the left (skating) knee bends deeply into the curve of the takeoff circle (figure 7.17a). The left arm is in front of the body and the right arm is in back. The shoulders remain square to the print as the left arm begins to open on the entry edge and, simultaneously and symmetrically with the right arm, strikes a square position in the air. The body weight on the takeoff edge rocks to the front of the blade, on the toe pick, as pressure is asserted against the ice for the liftoff, while simultaneously the left (skating) knee rises quickly and the right (free) leg stretches around in a wide circle with the body parallel to the ice (figure 7.17b).

LANDING

The landing is on a right back outside edge, passing over and toward the incoming edge and outside the circle of the takeoff edge in a back camel spin. The right knee is well bent on the landing and then straightens for the back camel with the left (free) leg extended and tension created between the right (skating) arm and the left foot to create balance and rotation (figure 7.17c). The weight of the body in the back spin balances over the ball of the foot. Once the back spin has been mastered, creative arm positions can be added. The spin is exited by rising into an open back spin position and finishing exactly as in a back scratch spin.

b

Figure 7.17 Flying camel: *(a)* Takeoff, *(b)* layout position, and *(c)* landing.

c

Training Tip

A frequent mistake is to rotate a full turn on the ice before taking off. The pressure to the front of the blade and the spring from the knee must be quick, allowing the rotation to occur in the air rather than on the ice. The takeoff is on a forward outside edge, not a back inside.

Standing sideways to the rink barrier, hold on with the left hand and jump to the right back camel position. Stand far enough away from the boards to allow room for the body to lean forward and still provide support during the jump. Practice and review back camel spins.

Flying Sit Spin

A flying sit takes off from a left forward outside edge, jumping into the air with the body striking a sit spin position before landing close to the point of takeoff.

PREPARATION

The preparation for a flying sit is identical to the preparation for a sit spin. It begins from back crossovers. The last right back inside edge is held with the left (free) leg extended behind the body in line with the right (skating) foot. Then the left leg steps into the circle on a strongly curving left forward outside edge, with the knee well bent and the shoulders level. The body weight should be aligned over the skating hip.

TAKEOFF

As the left foot steps forward on the outside edge, both the arms and the free leg extend behind the body before thrusting forward for the takeoff (figure 7.18a). The arms come from behind and drop close beside the body, then stretch forward. The motion is similar to the one used in an Axel takeoff (chapter 8). The left (skating) knee should be fully bent, then straightened on the takeoff. The right (free) foot helps accelerate the body into the air by swinging from back to front in a straight, diagonal line as the body turns counterclockwise into the spin. The body springs into the air and the left knee bends again, while airborne, into a tucked or sit spin position, while the right foot is extended out to the front in a sit spin position (figure 7.18b).

LANDING

The arms remain open and slightly out to the side as they come through before being brought forward for the landing. Once the peak is reached, the left foot extends down to absorb the force of the landing (figure 7.18c). The left foot lands on the toe pick and the knee bends to absorb the landing before lowering into the sit spin (figure 7.18d). The right (free) foot remains straight out in front in a position that is aligned in a straight line from the hip to the toe, parallel to the ice and level with the bent skating knee. The foot is turned out, and the back is straight but bent forward in about a 60-degree angle to the free leg. The landing edge should be close to and just ahead of the takeoff. The exit for a flying sit spin is identical to the exit for a sit spin.

a

b

c

d

Figure 7.18 The flying sit spin (a) takes off from a forward outside edge, (b) springs into the airborne sit spin position, (c) prepares for the landing, and (d) lowers into the sit spin position.

Practice the takeoff and landing at the rink barrier. Standing sideways to the boards, hold on with both hands and practice the timing of the left foot takeoff, tuck, and landing.

Death Drop

The death drop is a combination of a vertical flying camel spin on the takeoff and a back sit spin on the landing.

PREPARATION

The setup for a death drop is exactly the same as for a flying camel.

TAKEOFF

As the left forward outside edge is struck, both the arms and the free leg extend behind the body before thrusting forward for the takeoff. The arms should come from behind and drop close beside the body before stretching forward, similar to the motion used in an Axel takeoff (chapter 8). The left (skating) knee should be fully bent, then straightened on the takeoff as the body springs into the air. The right (free) foot helps accelerate the body into the air by swinging from back to front into a spread eagle or layout position almost parallel to the ice (figure 7.19a).

LANDING

As the right leg drops for the back sit position on the landing (figure 7.19b), the left leg extends behind the body in what could be momentarily described as a back spiral or camel position just before the body rotates into the back sit spin. The right (landing) toe hits the ice and then settles to the ball of the foot, and the right knee lowers into a back sit spin (figure 7.19c).

The arms should stretch out to the side in the air, landing like a flying camel spin. Check with the left arm forward, right arm back, then pull to a back sit. All previous instructions for the back sit spin apply. The death drop is exited by rising into an open back spin position and finishing exactly as in a back scratch spin.

Training Tip

Practice this spin, the three positions, and their transitions on the floor before taking the spin to the ice. Timing is critical.

a

b

c

Figure 7.19 The death drop takes off from a forward outside edge, *(a)* striking a layout position almost parallel to the ice, then *(b)* reaching for the ice with the right leg to prepare for the landing into *(c)* a back sit spin.

Master the Move

Lucinda Ruh's Dazzling Spins

Lucinda Ruh has mastered the technique of spinning, which is evident by the flexibility, positioning, and centering in this Biellmann spin.

Perhaps one of the best spinners in the world today is Switzerland's Lucinda Ruh. She recently gave the world notice with her perfect scores at the World Professional Championships. Ruh has not only mastered the technique of spinning, she has also invented new and interesting positions. Her flexibility, intricacy, and speed are dazzling. Spins do not always get the same credit as jumps, so when a skater like Ruh pays such minute attention to an underrated element, she distinguishes herself from other skaters and proves herself deserving of the world recognition she receives.

To reach Ruh's level of mastery, a skater must have technical precision. Spins should be fast, controlled, and centered; the hips and shoulders should be square; the skating foot should make small, even circles; and the body should be balanced over the blade to maintain momentum. If you've ever seen Ruh skate, you've probably noticed how her spins always remain in one spot. You also notice her unique arm and leg positions that make spins like the layback and Biellmann even more interesting and beautiful. Once you've perfected the fundamental technical elements, put your creative mind to work and try out different body positions. Improving your flexibility will also widen your creative options and improve your technique.

Combination Spins

A combination spin is a sequence of two or more spins linked together by changing feet or position without stopping rotation. Changing from one foot to the other, such as in a camel/back sit spin, constitutes a legal combination. It is also legal to remain on the same foot, as in a camel/forward sit spin. Advanced combinations link three or more spins together to create interesting, innovative spins. The following combination spins are common:

- Camel/back camel
- Sit/back sit or change sit
- Camel/sit
- Camel/layback
- Camel/layback/back sit
- Flying camel/back sit (when completed as a continuous action in the air, this combination becomes a death drop)

Problems occur in combination spins when the first spin is poorly executed, when speed is insufficient, or when the timing between the first and the second spin is poor. Opening the arms and free leg between spins is imperative to continue rotation on a combination spin. Each time the foot or position changes, it is necessary to open out and then pull in again to keep spinning.

In a well-executed combination spin the centering does not change. The print that remains on the ice should not move, but be traced over and over on the same spot. This continuity is achieved by opening the arms and the free foot while stepping from a front to a back spin. The free foot must be pigeon-toed (placed toe to toe) in front of the skating foot. At the same time the skating foot pushes away from the spin to place the free foot on the same spot that the skating foot formerly occupied.

Balance, control, and proper placement over the blade are necessary to achieve strong combination spins. Creativity is strongly encouraged and rewarded by the judges. To be of good quality, all spins in a combination should be equal in the strength of the spin and the number of rotations held. As with single spins each should be centered, controlled, and fast.

Teaching Tip

As with combination jumps, make sure the skater can execute each spin of the combination with sureness and consistency. When troubles occur in the combination, go back to the solo spins to make sure each one is solid. Then check for position and strength in the transition between the spins.

Illusions, Stars, and Butterflies

Because illusions, stars, and butterflies share a few common points, they are best learned in a progressive format. All of these elements are based on spinning principles and, because of their difficulty, should be learned only after good spin techniques are mastered.

Illusion

The illusion appears to be like a one-footed cartwheel. The body weight remains on one foot while the free foot swings around in a pinwheel action and, simultaneously, the body alternates between a forward position bent toward the ice and an upright position over the skating foot.

PREPARATION

Begin with a right back outside three, kicking the left (free) leg straight forward after the turn (figure 7.20a). Be careful that the foot is not kicked around in a circle but straight forward during the short right forward inside edge.

EXECUTION

The left (free) leg is brought down fast and passes very close to the right (skating) ankle during a second three turn, a right forward inside three. A second kick, following the second three, should be aimed in the exact same direction as the first kick. With enough rotation the free leg will be able to kick backward in a pendulum motion during the right back outside edge following the second turn.

The free leg must push powerfully backward, up, and around in the direction of the spin to keep the rotation going. The upper body goes forward and down on the right (skating) knee as the left (free) leg lifts high behind the body (figure 7.20b). When the left leg reaches the highest point behind the body, both legs must be very straight so the maximum extension can take place. To help the body bend forward during the back kick, the hand on the same side as the skating leg can reach for the ice. The knees must not be bent at this time.

As confidence increases the arm on the same side as the skating leg may go back and up in a circular motion during the front kick. The arm points straight up when the ankles are together and the skater is in the upright position. That same arm goes forward and down toward the ice during the back kick. Some skaters, however, prefer using the opposite arm. Exit on a right back outside edge (figure 7.20c).

Standing sideways next to the rink barrier, hold on with one hand and practice the opposing action of the free leg and the body position. When you begin this exercise, have a spotter stand at your side and make sure there are no other people standing directly in front of or behind you. Be sure to use the toe picks to catch the momentum of the action so that you do not slip off the front or back of the skate.

The section on illusions, stars, and butterflies was provided by Ann-Margareth Frei-Hall and edited by Carole Shulman. Frei-Hall was a three-time Swedish champion, the Scandinavian Champion in 1963-1964, and a World and Olympic competitor. Her coaching career began in Switzerland and South Africa before moving to the U.S. She currently resides in Vail, Colorado and holds a master rating in choreography and style.

a

b

Figure 7.20 Illusion: *(a)* After a small forward kick, the free foot swings down, then *(b)* backward in a pendulum motion. The finish position is shown in *(c)*.

c

Star

Think of the star as a forward outside three executed in a spiral position with the head, both hands, and both feet as points on the star.

PREPARATION

Both knees bend and the body leans forward before the left forward outside three. The toe of the right (free) leg pushes into the turn.

EXECUTION

The right (free) leg rises behind the body in a high spiral position immediately as it leaves the ice, reaching the highest point in the air in the middle of the three. The skating foot may lift off the ice if the spiral kick is strong and happens after the middle of the three.

As the body needs to be totally horizontal in a natural spiral position, the back must not arch during the kick; arching the back would be a tremendous, counter-productive strain. As in the back kick in the illusion, both knees must be very straight during the kicked spiral position. Likewise, the body needs to be lowered so that the free leg lifts high behind the skater. The arms stay outstretched to the sides during the star.

Again, as in the illusion, the free leg is kicked straight up; it only looks as though the leg goes around because the body is turning as the leg lifts. It is not possible to do a star if the free leg is slow and only reaches the highest point after the turn. As soon the three has been executed in the spiral position the right (free) leg comes down behind the left (skating) foot, and the toe presses into the ice to push into the next star.

It is not necessary to straighten the body after each star. Keeping a firm, forward body position allows faster turns with fewer adjustments. To obtain more speed going into the star, several fast *chaînés* (forward outside threes with a toe push) can be executed to generate better momentum, especially if the body is already leaning forward at the end of the second *chaîné*. Another variation is to end a star sequence with a couple of fast *chaînés* with the upper body upright over the skating foot.

A good way to begin learning the star is to use the rink barrier. Stand facing away from the barrier toward the center of the rink with your knees well bent. Then turn and hold the barrier with both hands as the free leg lifts up behind the body in a spiral position with both legs straightened. The body should lean forward with the back flat, not arched. Do this exercise in slow motion. Make certain the free leg is at the highest point in the middle of the three.

Butterfly

Butterflies can easily be learned after a flying camel spin is mastered. A butterfly is an aerial cartwheel in which the body position in the air is horizontal to the ice, as in a flying camel, but with an explosive arch of the back as the skater leaves the ice. (See figure 7.21 a-c.) For a flying camel the free leg reaches up to the side and slightly forward during the takeoff and then achieves a flat, spread-eagled position for a split second in the air. On the other hand, for a butterfly the free leg is kicked straight

a

b

c

Figure 7.21 Butterfly: *(a)* takeoff, *(b)* air position, and *(c)* landing.

backward during the takeoff and comes down as the other leg goes up in a scissor action. The landing is done in a back camel spin position.

Because of the difficulty of executing a butterfly, the exercises are listed first followed by instructions for the preparation and execution. These exercises should first be practiced off the ice and can be learned in four stages: exercise, preparation, execution, and landing.

At this point, don't worry about the body twist and release action. It is easier to add the twist later, after all the other elements have been learned. Take the time to make sure that each step is well mastered before moving on to the next exercise. Always go back a few steps if there is any confusion. Progressing slowly is much better than learning bad habits, which are more difficult to correct later.

Off-Ice Exercises

1. Backward French Can-Can

   Standing with your feet side by side, bend your knees slightly and kick first the right (landing) and then the left leg backward, changing legs in midair. Keep kicking one leg and then the other so that you are continuously changing legs. Both legs must be straight and strong in the air, and the arms must be solidly placed out to the sides at shoulder level. At this stage the body stays upright and the emphasis is on feeling the legs meet in midair. Repeat the exercise several times until the scissor action is mastered and consistent.

2. Single Scissor Action

   This exercise is similar to the backward French can-can but with only one change of foot. Always keep in mind to kick the landing leg backward first.

3. Barrel Position

   Stand with your feet shoulder-width apart. The knees should be bent so it looks as though you are sitting on a low stool or barrel. The arms are in a circle in front of the chest. From that position, open the arms firmly to the sides as you kick backward just as in the previous exercises, jumping into the scissor action. Do only one change of foot. This technique needs to be perfectly understood and mastered before moving on to the spiral jump.

4. Spiral Jump

   You must now get the upper body into a forward leaning position. From the perfect barrel position, tip the body forward horizontally as your arms go to the sides and you do the scissor action again. The landing will be in a back camel spin position with the body leaning forward, the left (free) leg extended, and the arms out to the side. The back must be strong so that there is no sagging on the landing. Once the body leans forward, it stays forward.

5. Hair-Raising Drop

   As timing is very important, you must stand up straight and try to lift both feet up at the same time and then drop quickly to the ice. This requires such speed that you will feel your hair rising from your head.

6. Moth in the Cocoon (not quite a butterfly yet, but close)

   Stand in the barrel position, but keep your body a little higher than before so that there will be a more sudden bending. Simultaneously bend both knees very fast (as in the hair-raising drop), lean forward, open the arms, kick back in a scissor action, and land in a back camel spin position. The feeling of simultaneously opening the arms to the sides while kicking the first leg backward will help your timing later when you do the butterfly. The moth in the cocoon should feel like a jumped spiral. The first right (free) leg kick in the air gives the jump the correct timing and height.

7. Body Twist (very advanced)
   Start in the barrel position with the upper body turned tightly to the right and most of the body weight on the right leg. As you start to lean forward, turn the upper body to the left and open the arms out to the side. Your chest should be leaning forward over a very bent left knee. Your feet will be very pigeon-toed (toe to toe) as the takeoff foot has not moved and is now turned in. Repeat this exercise slowly a few times without jumping, only feeling the torque of the upper body and the shift of the body weight from the right leg to the left toe, which should still be turned in. Finally, add the jump, always kicking the right leg straight backward. Never allow the right leg to come to the side.

On-Ice Exercises

Mastering the illusion, the star, and the off-ice exercises for butterflies is mandatory before beginning the butterfly on ice. At this stage, skaters stepping onto the ice are often excited to attempt the butterfly and may throw themselves uncontrollably into something that has never before been seen. This is the right time to review on ice what was practiced on the floor.

PREPARATION

Practice the following skills in order:

1. Standing in one place, walk high up on the toe picks to feel the traction and safe grip. The takeoff will be from the toes with no slipping or sliding.
2. Practice the backward French can-can on the ice, jumping from one toe to the other and kicking the free leg backward.
3. Using the barrel position exercise with the feet apart and parallel (no pigeon toe or spread eagle), sit on the imaginary barrel with arms in a circle in front. Stand in the middle of the blade with the body weight between the feet, and then shift the body weight to the left foot, rocking forward to the toe pick to jump. At the same time, kick the right leg high and backward while leaning forward and opening the arms out to the side. Land on the right toe in a back camel position. Remember, this is just a review of what was done on the floor.
4. A barrel spin can lend some rotation for those who are not yet ready for the torque and release action. Spin in the barrel position as fast as possible for at least five rotations. There should be no resistance from edges as the right blade will actually glide forward in a little circle and the left blade will glide backward on that same circle (about a foot in diameter).
5. Simulate the move while standing still. Review the takeoff again, pretending to be spinning in the barrel position. To create a true awareness, close your eyes and feel the shifting of the body weight from between the feet to the left toe, then open your eyes, jump, and change feet. Repeat this exercise several times. Keep it small and safe but technically perfect.
6. Practice the moth in the cocoon, which is almost a butterfly. Combine the barrel spin and takeoff, allowing a rotation of at least two turns before the

takeoff. Make sure you know which leg to kick backward first. The landing is identical to the landing for the flying camel.

If you are a little weak and tentative on the landing, do a few flying camels to recognize the feeling of the strong landing. Before going on to the butterfly, review again the takeoff and the difference between the flying camel and the butterfly. Once you are comfortable with this phase, add the tension and release action of the body twist.

7. Practice the body twist. Begin by standing still with the feet apart as in the barrel position. The arms should be open wide to the sides, but the upper body should be turned tightly to the right. The right arm is drawn as far back as possible, creating extreme tension. The body weight should be mostly on the right foot.

   Without the feet moving, the right hand is brought to the left one to rotate the body to the front and into the familiar barrel position, with the arms in a circle in front of the chest, the knees slightly bent, and the feet apart. The body weight should be midway between the two feet.

   With the feet still in the same position, the upper body continues to rotate to the left and starts to lean forward. The arms open when the upper body reaches the far left, and the body weight shifts to the left toe. That strange position should be held, with the feet still apart and pointing forward.

   Then in one continuous movement the body twists over the toe and the jump lifts off while the right leg kicks backward and the toe pushes away. The move is simply a scissor action and change of foot. It should be repeated several times, adding more knee bend (hair-raising drop) and more forward lean until the chest touches the left knee on the takeoff.

8. The skills in the previous section should be added to a fast barrel spin, allowing two rotations (at least) to prepare for the first position with the twist of the body to the right. Make sure the feet are about 12 inches apart for the barrel spin to allow the body weight to shift from right to left. The rotation should continue during the body transition from right to left.

   The right leg must kick straight backward for the takeoff, just as it does in a spiral. The power of that kick also determines timing and height, since the jump must occur at the exact moment when the leg goes up. The takeoff is from the toe; although the feet are in fact parallel, they will feel as though they are turned in since they did not change position while the body rotated from right to left during the spin. The jump lands in a strong back camel spin position.

EXECUTION

Once the previous skills are mastered, speed can be added. The pattern of the tracing will form a reverse $ sign: two half circles, each with a radius of about five feet, with a straight line (or long axis) running lengthwise through the half circles.

Both feet glide on the first half circle, with the right foot in front of the left. The right arm is strongly extended to the back, and the left arm is in front over the tracing. On entering the second half circle, the body weight shifts to the right foot on a forward inside edge with a well-bent knee. The left foot (with a straight knee) drags on the ice behind the right foot. The upper body is leaning forward over the right knee, parallel to the ice and the right arm is still strongly extended to the back. Only the body weight is over the line of axis. The legs stop on the long axis, facing the starting point. A barrel spin is now executed on the axis with a few revolutions and strong upper body tension, and then the body rotates to the left and the jump takes off from the left toe.

The process should be repeated, this time without stopping on the long axis before spinning. A few revolutions should be turned before jumping. To improve timing, the spin should begin on medium bent knees and then drop to a deep knee bend just before the takeoff. The body should remain low and parallel to the ice through the landing in a camel spin position.

As proficiency increases, the barrel spin becomes shorter and shorter until all the moves can be done in order, holding the tension until only half a barrel turn is needed. At this point, the upper body should be thrown from one side of the line to the other very quickly. The rotation comes from throwing the body forcefully from right to left in a circular motion. The right arm must stay behind until the last second. During the butterfly, the arms should be stretched out to the side and stable.

The butterfly is a spectacular element in skating. It can be enhanced by combining several butterflies, one after the other, ending in a back camel spin.

Summary

All skills look easy when they're done well. Spins are often underrated when compared to jumps, but without the balance spins provide in a program a skater would be boring to watch and the program incomplete. In recent years spins have begun to receive welcome attention, and skaters are now being rewarded for the difficulty and ingenuity of their spins.

chapter 8
Jumps

Jumps continue to be the central focus of freestyle skating. No matter the number of elements added or the emphasis placed on spirals, spins, and footwork, jumps are the single most impressive element of any freestyle performance. How these jumps are performed may vary, but there is common ground that supports all good jumping techniques. With the basic techniques explained here, you should be better prepared to adopt the specific techniques that are right for you.

Determining the Direction of Rotation

Before beginning to jump, it is important to determine which direction to rotate in the air—clockwise (to the right) or counterclockwise (to the left). Most skaters figure out their natural rotation without any assistance. Others are confused and jump first one way and then the other, and some will jump in one direction and spin in the other. It is imperative for a beginning skater to always jump and spin in the same direction.

There are several ways to determine direction of rotation. The direction seldom relates to whether the skater is right- or left-handed. The important step is to determine which leg is the strongest; that will decide the landing foot since all basic jumps are landed on the same foot. The stronger leg can be identified by checking to see which is used to kick a ball or which foot is used first to climb a stair.

If both legs appear to be equally strong, then determine which turning direction provides the most natural rotation. A coach or parent can help identify the most natural direction by asking the skater to move away and then calling the skater's name and noting the direction in which the skater turns to respond.

Sometimes it is necessary to repeat these exercises several times to determine consistency, especially with skaters who might be ambidextrous. In any case, beginning skaters must not jump and spin in opposite directions. There is a strong advantage to rotating to the left since that is the direction most often used by skaters and is the natural directional flow used in all rinks. Skaters who are inclined to jump or spin in both directions should wait until all the basics have been learned before introducing the alternate rotation.

Jumping Fundamentals

There are four key parts to a jump:

1. Preparation
2. Takeoff
3. Rotation (air position)
4. Landing

Precise timing is critical in all of these parts. Each body movement must be done at an exact time and place. To create good rhythm and timing, all of the body parts must

Sections of this chapter have been reprinted, with permission, from the *PSA Coaches Manual*, 1999.

The section on jumping fundamentals was provided by Kathy Casey. Casey is a World and Olympic coach with over 30 years of coaching experience. She has taught numerous national and international champions and holds a master rating in figures and freestyle, dance and free dance, as well as a senior rating in pairs.

work harmoniously together. All jumps share the fundamental techniques that follow. Understanding these fundamentals is the first step toward developing the timing and rhythm needed for good execution.

Preparation

Body preparation entails precisely what the body, arms, and legs do to prepare for the jump. Each jump has its own specific positions, movements, and patterns that must be done in preparation for the actual jump. It's important to understand these positions and movements clearly and to do them correctly and exactly the same every time. A good rhythm in the jump preparation is also important as it assists in proper liftoff. One common error to watch out for is rotating the shoulders and hips before the jump. Also, remember that the back must always be kept straight when going into any jump.

Takeoff

The knees are the main explosive force in a jump. They are assisted by the arms, ankles, feet, upper body, head, and correct body alignment. To get maximum height, the body must be straight and must not rotate excessively before the jump.

Correct rhythm and timing between all body parts is very important. On toe jumps, in which the toe pick is used to give extra height, the timing between the skating leg and the toe tap is critical. Figure 8.1a illustrates the phases of the double toe loop, including the toe tap on takeoff. On edge jumps, in which the jump takes off from one of the four edges of the skate, the skating knee must bend before jumping and then extend to a straight leg on the takeoff. The toe pick should be the last contact with the ice. Figure 8.1b illustrates the phases of the double Axel, which takes off from a forward outside edge.

Rotation

The toe tap initiates rotation on toe jumps, while the increase of curve on the takeoff edge begins the rotation on edge jumps. While preparation and takeoff differ from jump to jump, the position in the air is the same for all jumps. In the air the body rotates on an axis; it must be straight from the head to the toes. (See figure 8.1a-b.) The legs should be straight and tightly crossed at the ankles with the knees and feet facing straight ahead. The hips and shoulders should be level and square. A wrapped free leg is undesirable and is caused mainly by premature rotation of the shoulders and hips. The tightness of the arms and free leg depends on the number of rotations to be done. The greater the number of rotations, the tighter the arms and legs must be.

Landing

Checking, or stopping rotation, is necessary to land a jump properly. It is achieved by quickly extending the arms and free leg into their landing positions. Landing positions may vary but must be executed with the hips square, the free leg extended, and the upper body strong. (See figure 8.1a-b.) It's essential to land on the toe of the blade and then remain balanced over the ball of the foot for maximum glide on a strong back outside edge. A quiet, smooth landing edge that is not on a tight curve is also important.

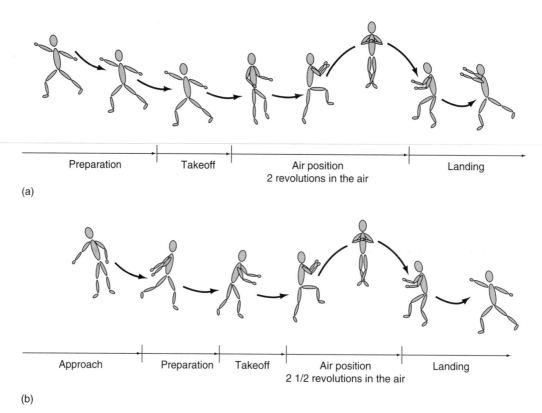

(a)

Preparation | Takeoff | Air position 2 revolutions in the air | Landing

(b)

Approach | Preparation | Takeoff | Air position 2 1/2 revolutions in the air | Landing

Figure 8.1 Jump phases of the *(a)* double toe loop and *(b)* double Axel. While the preparation and takeoff positions differ from jump to jump, the air position and landing are the same for all jumps. The only difference is the tightness of the body in the air, depending on the number of rotations.

A good landing position has a softly bent knee to cushion the weight of the landing, a stretched and extended free foot with the free leg turned out, a straight back, a raised head, and arms extended out to the side. Arm positions vary slightly depending on style and variations used to gain control and correct overrotation.

Jumping Progression

Viewing the world of jumps from different perspectives is useful. When learning, teaching, or taking a rating exam, you may choose to categorize jumps according to the takeoff. These are sometimes referred to as families of jumps.

Edge jumps: bunny hop, waltz jump, Axel, Salchow, loop, Walley

Toe jumps: split, flip, toe loop, Lutz, toe Walley, stag jump

Jumps that take off and land on the same foot: loop, flip, Lutz

Jumps that change feet: bunny hop, waltz jump, Axel, Salchow, toe loop

Categorizing jumps allows you to recognize the similarities and differences in execution. This can be of great value to coaches when explaining jumps to skaters and helping their bodies feel the jumps.

Coaches should have a progression in mind when teaching jumps. The bunny hop is often the first jump introduced to beginning skaters. Most skaters are able to do this jump off either foot. The bunny hop is a good introduction to the waltz jump as the takeoff and springing action used in the bunny hop are also used in waltz jumps and later in Axels. Repeated bunny hops covering the length of the rink strengthen the jumping leg and help with the timing of the arms and free leg. Jumps with half rotations are valuable in teaching the action and timing needed for single jumps. The order for teaching single jumps is usually Salchow, toe loop, loop, flip, and Lutz, but there are no hard and fast rules. Small jumps such as mazurkas and falling leaves help establish a rhythm in jumping and help develop footwork and jumping sequences.

Teaching Tip

Teach jumps in an organized and thoughtful manner. Each jump should not only be related to other jumps in specific ways but also be developed with a particular pattern and setup. Skaters can be taught the rhythm pattern and setup on half jumps and carry this knowledge through singles, doubles, triples, and quads.

As with the spins, all descriptions are based on a skater who rotates to the left, or counterclockwise. Skaters who rotate to the right must reverse the starting foot and direction.

Bunny Hop

The bunny hop is a great beginning jump. Children delight in its name and it involves no edges, no rotation, and the comfort of a two-part landing. It is like a little skip. The bunny hop takes off from the right foot, then steps on the left toe and finishes on the right foot. This jump can easily be done beginning with the left foot instead of the right.

PREPARATION

Begin with a two-footed forward glide when the jump is first introduced. As confidence increases, begin with a one-footed glide.

TAKEOFF

The left foot picks up and swings first backward (figure 8.2a) and then through to the front (figure 8.2b) to propel a forward motion as the right foot rocks to the toe for the liftoff (figure 8.2c).

LANDING

The left toe lands on the ice followed quickly by a right forward glide (figure 8.2d). The exchange of the left and right feet simulates a scissor action. There is no rotation in a bunny hop. Because this is a forward jump (i.e., not done on a curve), no edge is noted.

Try a two-footed jump from a standing position. With a spotter close by, bend both knees, do a small jump straight up into the air, and return to the ice on two feet. Make sure you land on the toe picks of both blades. The purpose of this exercise is to make you comfortable with leaving and returning to the ice.

Next, rehearse a walkthrough of the bunny hop at the rink barrier, holding on with one hand. To visualize the action of the jump, imagine you are stepping over a puddle.

Figure 8.2 Bunny hop: *(a)* The left leg swings backward, then *(b)* extends forward. *(c)* The right foot rocks to the toe for pushoff, *(d)* followed by a right forward glide.

Half Jumps

A half jump is so named because one half turn is executed in the air before landing. Most always it is a half turn from backward to forward. An ideal way to begin learning jumps is to start with a few half jumps before beginning jumps with full rotation. It is not necessary to learn all of these half jumps at the beginning. These jumps add interest and variety both for beginning skaters and later in programs where choreography or a musical accent is appropriate.

Mazurka

A mazurka feels a bit like a sideways bunny hop since the takeoff and scissoring free foot action are the same. Whereas the body position for the takeoff of a bunny hop is square to the print, in a mazurka it is parallel, or sideways.

PREPARATION

Begin with a left forward outside three. From the back edge of the three, the left foot provides the push off to step onto a right back outside edge (figure 8.3a), and the left toe is placed into the ice with the body facing parallel to the direction of movement. Another method is to take off from a back inside edge.

TAKEOFF AND ROTATION

As the body weight is transferred from the right back outside edge to the left toe, the left knee is bent, then straightens to elevate the body into the air and at the same time, the right (free) foot swings across the left foot in a scissor action so that the feet are actually crossed in the air with the right foot in front and the left foot behind (figure 8.3b). The arms should be held out to the side with the head erect and the back straight.

LANDING

The jump is landed on the left toe (figure 8.3c) followed by a quick right forward inside edge, which is often followed by a forward inside three turn. The exit three turn assists in controlling the awkwardness of a forward inside edge landing.

Once the jump has been mastered, arm positions in the air can be creatively varied. Olympic champion Tenley Albright varied the scissor action of this jump by crossing her free foot behind instead of in front.

From a standstill position, turn sideways and practice the scissoring action of the free foot, stepping left, right, left.

a

b

Figure 8.3 Mazurka: *(a)* Preparation, *(b)* scissor action in the air, and *(c)* landing.

c

Ballet Jump

The ballet jump is named for its beautiful position in the air, which traditionally has the left arm overhead and the right arm out to the side with the skating foot straight beneath the body and the free leg out to the side. The air position can be varied.

PREPARATION

From a right back outside edge with the body facing parallel to the print, the left toe is placed on the ice (figure 8.4a).

TAKEOFF AND ROTATION

As the left toe is placed into the ice for the takeoff, the left knee bends so that the body can be lifted into the air for the jump. The ballet position is instantly struck in the air position before landing (figure 8.4b).

LANDING

Landing is done on the left toe. Just as with the mazurka jump, an inside three turn on the exit will assist in controlling the right forward inside edge landing.

Once the jump has been mastered, the positions of the arms in the air can be creatively varied.

▪ Practice walking through the jump before trying it at speed.

a

b

Figure 8.4   Ballet jump: *(a)* Preparation, and *(b)* air position.

Half Flip Hop

The half flip hop is a preparatory jump to learning a flip. It is a one half turn whereas a flip is a whole turn.

PREPARATION

Begin with a left forward outside three.

TAKEOFF AND ROTATION

The right toe is placed on the ice (figure 8.5a) and the feet are drawn together as the body lifts into the air and rotates one half turn (figure 8.5b).

LANDING

The jump lands on the right toe (figure 8.5c), and then the left foot steps forward on an outside edge (figure 8.5d).

Half Flip

The half flip varies from the half flip hop in that the takeoff and landing are on opposite feet, whereas the hop is executed on the same foot.

PREPARATION

Begin with a left forward outside three.

TAKEOFF AND ROTATION

The right toe is placed on the ice (figure 8.6a) and the feet are drawn together as the body lifts into the air and rotates one half turn (figure 8.6b), just as in the half flip hop.

LANDING

The jump lands on the left toe (figure 8.6c), and then the right foot steps forward on an inside edge.

A good exercise for both the half flip and the half flip hop is to hold onto the rink barrier and practice the takeoff toe and landing action.

a   b

c   d

Figure 8.5 The half flip hop *(a)* vaults off the right toe, *(b)* rotates one half turn, *(c)* lands on the right toe, and *(d)* finishes with a left forward glide.

a

b

c

Figure 8.6 The half flip (a) takes off from the right toe, (b) rotates one half turn, lands on the left toe, and (c) steps forward onto a right foot glide.

Half Loop

This jump begins with the body moving backward on a left back outside edge. It rotates one half turn in the air, landing on the right back inside edge.

PREPARATION

Following a right forward outside three turn, the right foot pushes off onto a left back outside edge on a well-bent knee. The right arm is in front, the left arm is behind, and the right (free) foot is in front over the print (figure 8.7a). Make sure the body stays square over the takeoff edge without pushing the skating hip too far into the circle.

TAKEOFF AND ROTATION

The left (skating) knee bends and the upper body begins to rotate (figure 8.7b). The left arm moves toward the right as the knee straightens for the takeoff. During the jump the right (free) foot remains in front in preparation for the landing.

a

b

c

Figure 8.7   The half loop *(a)* takes off from a left back outside edge, *(b)* rotates one half turn, and *(c)* lands on a right back inside edge.

LANDING

The rotation of the arms should continue through the jump so that the left arm finishes forward and the right arm back when the jump lands on the right back inside edge (figure 8.7c).

Practice a two-footed landing before attempting to land on one foot.

Falling Leaf

This jump begins with the body moving backward on a right back outside edge. It rotates one half turn in the air with the legs in an open position, landing on the left toe and then stepping forward onto a right inside edge.

PREPARATION

Starting from a left forward outside three turn, the left foot pushes off onto a right back outside edge on a well-bent knee. The left arm is in front, the right arm is behind, and the left (free) foot is in front over the print.

TAKEOFF AND ROTATION

Beginning from the well-bent right (skating) knee, the body jumps straight into the air as the left (free) foot sweeps from the forward position into an open or nearly split position before landing. See figure 8.8.

Figure 8.8   Air position in the falling leaf jump.

LANDING

The left toe lands on the ice, followed by the right forward inside edge.

Training Tip

Practice the mechanics of the jump until you feel comfortable before adding the open position.

Half Lutz Hop

This jump is the same as the half flip except that the takeoff is from a back outside edge instead of the back inside. The right toe is placed on the ice and one half rotation is turned in the air before the jump lands on the right toe followed by a left forward outside edge.

PREPARATION

The half Lutz hop begins from left back crossovers. The left back outside edge is held, and then the right toe is placed on the ice and the feet are drawn together as the body lifts into the air.

TAKEOFF AND ROTATION

The body rotates one half turn before landing.

LANDING

The jump lands on the right toe and then steps onto a left forward outside edge.

Half Lutz

This jump is the same as the half flip except that the takeoff is from a back outside edge instead of the back inside. The right toe is placed on the ice and one half rotation is turned in the air. The jump lands on the left toe followed by a right forward inside edge.

PREPARATION

Begin from left back crossovers by holding the left back outside edge.

TAKEOFF AND ROTATION

The right toe is placed on the ice and the feet are drawn together as the body lifts into the air and rotates one half turn before landing.

LANDING

The left toe lands on the ice, and then the right foot steps onto a forward inside edge.

Before executing the half Lutz hop and the half Lutz, hold onto the rink barrier and practice the takeoff toe and landing action.

Edge Jumps

Edge jumps are those that take off from one of the four edges used by each foot (forward outside, forward inside, back outside, and back inside). Most skaters prefer either toe jumps or edge jumps. Body type, coaching methods, and learning style influence each skater's preference. Edge jumps are more flowing because there is no interruption on the takeoff, whereas toe jumps require a vaulting action precipitated by the toe.

Waltz Jump

The waltz jump is a half turn rotation in the air. It takes off on the left forward outside edge and lands on the right back outside edge. A jump that is seldom performed today is a one-footed waltz jump, where the takeoff and landing are done on the same foot with an outside edge takeoff and an inside edge landing. This is sometimes referred to as a three jump.

PREPARATION

The waltz jump begins on a curve with a left forward outside three turn. The right foot steps backward on a strong back outside edge and then the left foot steps forward for the takeoff.

TAKEOFF AND ROTATION

The left knee bends and the right (free) leg and both arms extend behind the body (figure 8.9a). The body weight rises up off the knee as the free foot swings forward and into the air. The body follows through and the arms lift to assist in gaining height. Leading slightly with the left arm on the rise of the jump prevents excessive rotation. As in all jumps that take off in a forward direction, the blade rocks from back of center to front, and the toe pick is the last part of the blade to leave the ice. At the peak of the jump the legs should be in a semi-split or open position with the knees straight and the arms extended out to the side (figure 8.9b). The body weight is centered in its shift from the takeoff to the landing edge.

LANDING

After the body weight shifts onto the landing foot, the toe pick is the first part of the blade to touch the ice before the foot rolls back to the ball of the foot to maintain a flowing back outside edge (figure 8.9c).

Stand perpendicular to the rink barrier, holding on with your left hand and standing on your left foot. Jump forward one half turn, changing hands on the boards and landing backward on the right foot. Repeat this exercise several times before leaving the boards. Once away from the boards, practice a two-footed jump from front to back before attempting to do a one-footed jump.

a

b

c

Figure 8.9 Waltz jump: *(a)* Takeoff, *(b)* half turn rotation in an open air position, and *(c)* landing.

Salchow

The Salchow is named for the Swedish world champion Ulrich Salchow. It begins from a back inside edge and ends on a back outside edge. Sometimes it is referred to as a waltz jump from a back inside edge, which is almost true except that a waltz jump is one half rotation and the Salchow is one full revolution.

a

PREPARATION

The entry into the jump is begun by a left forward outside three. This time there is no change of feet following the three, as the jump will originate from the left back inside edge of the three. Work on checking the shoulders after the three to establish control and set up the momentum of the jump (figure 8.10a).

TAKEOFF AND ROTATION

The right (free) arm moves with the right (free) foot, which is behind the skating foot after the three. Both the free arm and the free foot should be brought forward as the knee bends in preparation for the jump (figure 8.10b). Pressure is maintained on the front of the blade as the free leg and free arm move in a circular pattern around the skating side (figure 8.10c) and into the air position.

b

c

Figure 8.10 Preparation and takeoff positions in the Salchow: (a) Establish control after the left forward outside three, (b) the right (free) foot is brought forward, then (c) the free leg moves in a circular pattern around the skating side and the jump takes off from the left back inside edge. The focus is kept on the positions of the feet during preparation and takeoff since these are the phases that differ from jump to jump.

The toe pick is the last part of the blade to leave the ice. Rotation is created as the hips come around to face the direction of travel and the body weight changes in the air from the left back inside takeoff edge to the landing on the right back outside edge.

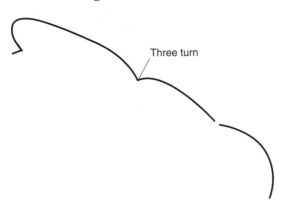

Three turn

Figure 8.11 Print on the ice resulting from a Salchow takeoff.

LANDING

Again, the toe pick is first to touch the ice before balancing to the ball of the foot on a strong backward glide.

It's important to practice the preparation for the jump, including the three on a straight line. After the turn remain on the line and execute the jump, working on control and balance. Figure 8.11 illustrates the print on the ice after a well-executed Salchow takeoff.

Loop

The loop jump begins from a right back outside edge, jumping into the air and rotating one full revolution before landing on the same edge as the takeoff—the right back outside.

The air position of the loop jump is the basic position for body and balance in all multi-rotation jumps. Fritz Dietl named the loop the king of jumps. It used to be known as the Rittberger.

PREPARATION

There are three common preparations for this jump:

1. A left forward outside three and then a step down onto the right back outside edge
2. A right forward inside three ending on the right back outside edge
3. A right forward inside Mohawk and then a step down onto the right back outside edge

From the back outside edge, while the free foot is trailing in front of the takeoff edge, the right knee bends (figure 8.12a); the right arm is placed behind the body and the left arm in front. Make sure the body stays square over the takeoff edge without pushing the skating hip too far into the circle. The shoulders, hips, and foot should all be aligned.

Timing is critical on any jump. Whether you use a 1–2–3 count or words such as "hold—bend—jump," establishing the rhythm is important.

TAKEOFF AND ROTATION

The jump is begun by straightening the knee and rotating the upper body to leave the ice (figure 8.12 b-c). The right arm moves toward the left and the arms pull together in the air. During the jump the free foot remains in front with the legs slightly crossed. (This position becomes more pronounced as rotations increase.)

a

b

Figure 8.12 Preparation and takeoff positions in the loop jump: *(a)* From a right back outside edge, *(b)* the knee begins to straighten in order to *(c)* begin takeoff and rotation.

c

LANDING

On the landing the free foot lifts slightly and then extends back for the right back outside edge landing position.

Practice the takeoff and landing positions without rotation. Jump up in place with the free foot in front and the arms in. Then land with the free foot lifting from the front and extending back and the arms stretched out. Repeat this exercise several times. Practice first on the floor and then with a spotter on the ice until you understand the balance well. A straight line preparation is helpful to correct an overrotated takeoff.

Walley

This jump is named for Nate Walley. It is executed from a right back inside edge, lifting off and rotating one full turn in the air before landing on a right back outside edge.

PREPARATION

Two common methods are used. One is a chain of back inside-outside-inside changes of edge where the last back inside edge is held and the free foot is extended behind the skating foot just before the takeoff. The other is a left forward outside three followed by a step down on the right back inside edge for the takeoff. On either entry, use a strong checked position with the left arm in front of the body and right arm behind. The left (free) foot is extended and crossed behind the right (skating) foot, outside the line of tracing (figure 8.13a). The right (skating) knee is bent.

a

b

c

Figure 8.13 Preparation and takeoff positions in the Walley: *(a)* During the entry, the free foot is crossed behind the skating foot. *(b)* The free foot then kicks out to the side, and *(c)* the body begins to rotate counterclockwise and spring into the air off the back inside edge.

TAKEOFF AND ROTATION

The momentum of the liftoff is generated by the left (free) foot kicking from behind the skating foot and out to the side (figure 8.13b) as the arms and the skating knee lift up while the body begins to rotate counterclockwise (figure 8.13c). The jump springs into the air from a right back inside edge as the right (skating) foot pushes away from the ice. The body weight must be firmly centered over the right side for the takeoff. The left (free) leg in the air is in an open position, parallel to the right foot and hip-width away. The arms pull in across the chest and open out for the landing.

LANDING

The landing is done on a right back outside edge.

Practice alternate jumping side-to-side from a right back inside edge to a left back inside edge without rotation to strengthen the takeoff edge. Also practice jumping a right back inside counter to learn the placement of the weight over the right side on the takeoff.

Axel

This jump is named for Norwegian Axel Paulsen, who invented the jump in 1882. It was first performed in a competition in Vienna, Austria. In its day it was the most difficult jump ever performed. The Axel is considered a single jump, but it is actually one and one-half revolutions in the air. Before an Axel is attempted the following should be accomplished:

- All single jumps landed soundly
- Single jump combinations landed with balance and strength; i.e., flip/loop, loop/loop, Lutz/loop, and waltz/loop
- Backspins executed strongly

The Axel is one of very few jumps that take off on a forward edge. It starts on the left forward outside edge, rotates one and a half turns in the air, and lands on the right back outside edge.

PREPARATION

The most common preparation is a left forward outside three turn, stepping back on a right back outside edge and then stepping forward on the left outside edge. Forward outside swing rolls can also be used as a preparation for this jump. (In a forward outside swing roll the free leg begins backward, then swings to the front. The action is reversed on a backward swing roll.) Another variation is to enter the jump from back crossovers, stepping down on a right back outside edge before turning forward on the left foot for the outside edge takeoff.

TAKEOFF AND ROTATION

The arms and the free leg are extended behind the body on the left forward outside takeoff edge (figure 8.14). The skating knee is well bent. The extended free leg is held solidly in back to control excessive rotation before the jump. On the takeoff the free leg must swing straight through, not around. The knee of the free leg is

Figure 8.14   The Axel takes off from a forward outside edge.

Figure 8.15   Print on the ice resulting from a well-executed Axel takeoff.

bent, as shown in figure 8.14. There is a slight skid or scrape on the takeoff edge, which will increase as rotation increases for the double or triple jump. The skid should be kept to a minimum but will vary depending on the weight and size of the skater and the speed going into the jump. Too much skid affects the quality of the jump, in which case the body position and early rotation must be corrected. Figure 8.15 illustrates the print on the ice resulting from a well-executed Axel takeoff.

The left foot rolls up to the toe pick and springs into the air as simultaneously the left knee straightens and the right knee and arms thrust forward to help get the jump to its full height. The arms pass close to the body from back to front, bending at the elbows.

The air position for the Axel is the same as for the loop jump. By the time the apex of the jump is reached, the body has turned one half rotation. The body weight shifts from the left (takeoff) foot to the right (landing) foot. The arms should pull in across the center of the chest with the elbows down. The left leg should be crossed in front of the right, slightly above the ankle, and the left hip should be slightly lifted. The position of the head is optional. It can either be slightly rotated toward the left or remain straight ahead.

LANDING

For the landing, the left knee lifts slightly up and then passes in a straight line close by the right (landing) leg. The arms open up and break out, pushing back to a checked landing position. The right knee is well bent and the left (free) leg is extended fully behind.

A good practice jump is the waltz/loop combination, which will illustrate the action of an Axel in the air and help you understand that an Axel is a combination of the waltz and loop jumps. The back spin with a strong exit illustrates the air position and landing action of an Axel.

Another good practice exercise is to do several single loop jumps in a row. This exercise will help you feel a tighter body position, which is needed in the rotation of the Axel.

A third common exercise is a bell jump, which is an Axel executed with just one rotation and landed forward on two feet. The purpose of this exercise is to feel the body and air positions without having to concentrate on the landing.

Toe Jumps

As previously explained, toe jumps are those that use the vaulting action of the toe to assist in the takeoff. Like a pole-vaulter's pole, the toe helps to create lift, which can result in a very dynamic jump.

Split Jump

This jump must be entered and executed with speed. Take off from a left back inside edge, placing the right toe into the ice and turn one half rotation in the air with the legs in a split position. Land on the left toe and then step onto a right forward inside edge.

PREPARATION

Begin with a right forward inside Mohawk.

TAKEOFF AND ROTATION

From the back edge, the right toe is placed into the ice and the feet are drawn together, bringing the left foot through and forward into the air in a split position. A great deal of knee bend is required on the takeoff to get the elevation and timing for the split to occur. The left leg, which is in front for the split, should be turned out and the right leg (behind) turned in—the same placement that would be used to do the splits on the floor. Both toes should be pointed. The takeoff and landing is a scissor action that begins with the left toe in the ice and ends on the left toe before stepping on the right forward inside edge. The arms should be left out to the side for the beginning skater, but with skill and practice the arm positions may be varied.

LANDING

As with all forward inside edge landings, it is common to follow through with a forward inside three to a back outside edge.

A common variation of the split jump is the Russian split, in which the body does not turn to the front in the air but faces to the side with each hand reaching toward a foot. (See figure 8.16.) When done well, this is a spectacular jump that demonstrates great agility.

Figure 8.16   Russian split.

The most important factor is to acquire the flexibility needed for the split. Practice the splits on the floor. Also stand at the barrier and practice the feel of the split in the air, using the support of your arms on the boards to delay the quick action of the jump that takes place on the ice.

Stag Jump

The stag jump is very similar to the split jump except that the front leg is bent at the knee and brought under the body in a stag position. This jump takes off from a left back inside edge, placing the right toe into the ice and turning one-half rotation in the air with the legs parallel to the ice in a stag position. Land on the left toe followed by a right forward inside edge.

PREPARATION

Begin with a right forward inside Mohawk.

TAKEOFF AND ROTATION

The takeoff is the same as for the split jump; the only change is the body's position in the air. From the back edge, the right toe is placed into the ice and the feet are drawn together, bringing the left foot forward in a bent knee position up and under the body (figure 8.17). The right leg remains extended behind the body in a straight, horizontal position. The arm positions can be varied depending on skill and creativity.

LANDING

The landing is the same as for the split jump.

Figure 8.17   Stag jump.

Practice the stag position by jumping up in place and hitting the correct position in the air before landing. Also stand at the boards and practice the feel of the stag while using the support of your arms on the boards to delay the quick action of the jump that takes place on the ice. You may need to use a spotter.

Toe Loop

The toe loop takes off from a right back outside edge assisted by a toe tap from the left foot. It makes one revolution in the air before landing on a right back outside edge.

PREPARATION

The most common entry is from a right forward inside three: the back outside edge of the turn is held, and the left toe is placed into the ice for the takeoff. Another entry is from a left forward outside drop three: the left toe is placed into the ice after the turn for the takeoff.

TAKEOFF AND ROTATION

As the left toe goes into the ice on the takeoff (figure 8.18), the right foot pulls toward the left toe while the left arm extends forward in front of the body and the right arm back. The right knee bends in preparation for the takeoff and continues to draw past the left toe. The momentum of the legs and arms vaults the body into the air for one full revolution. The arms pull in and across the chest and then open out for the landing.

LANDING

Land the jump on a right back outside edge.

It's important to practice the pulling action of the takeoff by placing the left toe in the ice and drawing the right foot beside the left. Watch the placement of the toe pick; if it's placed too far to the side it will cause a twisted, prematurely rotated jump. Figure 8.19 illustrates the print on the ice that results from a well-executed toe loop.

Figure 8.18   The toe loop takes off from a right back outside edge, placing the left toe into the ice.

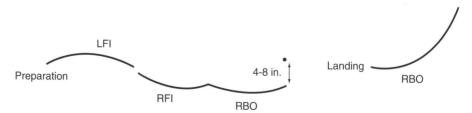

LFI

Preparation

4-8 in.

Landing

RBO

RFI

RBO

Figure 8.19   The print on the ice resulting from a well-executed toe loop.

Toe Walley

A toe Walley is executed from a right back inside edge by placing the left toe in the ice, lifting off, and rotating one full turn in the air before landing on a right back outside edge. The difference between a toe loop and a toe Walley is that the toe loop takes off from a back outside edge and the toe Walley takes off from a back inside edge.

PREPARATION

The toe Walley begins with a left forward outside three followed by a step down on the right back inside edge. The arms should be in a strong checked position with the left arm in front of the body and right arm behind. The left toe is placed in the ice for the takeoff. The right (skating) knee is bent.

TAKEOFF AND ROTATION

As the left toe is placed in the ice the right foot pulls toward the left toe (figure 8.20). The left arm continues to extend forward and the right arm back. The right knee bends in preparation for the takeoff and continues to draw past the left toe, using the momentum of the leg action and arms to project the body into the air for one full revolution. The arms pull in and across the chest and then open out for the landing.

LANDING

The landing is done on a right back outside edge.

Figure 8.20 Takeoff position in the toe Walley. The left toe is placed into the ice and the jump takes off from a right back inside edge.

Practice jumping from the right back inside edge to the left back inside edge without rotation to feel the action of the takeoff. Remember to remain on the back inside edge at all times.

Flip

The flip jump is executed by skating on a left back inside edge and placing the right toe into the ice to lift off and rotate one full turn. It lands on a right back outside edge. The print on the ice after a well-executed flip takeoff is illustrated in figure 8.21.

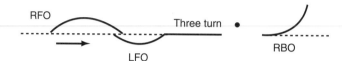

RFO

Three turn •

LFO

RBO

Figure 8.21   The print on the ice resulting from a well-executed flip jump.

PREPARATION

Either a left forward outside three or a right forward inside Mohawk can be executed in preparation for this jump. The turn must not swing wide but rather be performed on more of a straight line. In a well-executed flip the right (free) leg reaches low and straight behind the body with the body weight over the left (skating) foot. The back should be straight but slightly inclined forward with the shoulders level. The left arm should be in front of the body over the print, and the right arm should be behind.

TAKEOFF AND ROTATION

The left foot draws toward the right, transferring the weight over the right foot for the takeoff (figure 8.22). Both arms pull down and then up and in toward the body. In the air the right leg should be straight and the left leg crossed slightly over in front of the right, with the left hip slightly lifted and the body weight still over the right side. The arms should be close to the body at chest level for one full revolution. The left knee lifts slightly out and the arms open before pushing back to a checked landing position.

LANDING

The flip jump lands on the right back outside edge.

Figure 8.22   The flip jump takes off from a left back inside edge, placing the right toe into the ice.

Standing on two feet, jump up and turn one revolution, landing again on two feet. Draw the arms in on the rotation and out for the landing. Make sure a spotter is close by until your balance is secure.

Lutz

The Lutz jump is exactly like the flip except that the takeoff edge is a back outside instead of a back inside edge. The Lutz jump is executed by skating on a left back outside edge, placing the right toe into the ice, lifting off, and rotating one full turn before landing on a right back outside edge. The print on the ice resulting from a well-executed Lutz jump is illustrated in figure 8.23.

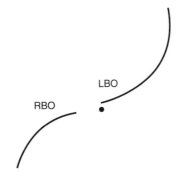

LBO

RBO

Figure 8.23 The print on the ice left after a well-executed Lutz jump.

PREPARATION

The Lutz is most commonly entered by doing back crossovers and then holding the left back outside edge in preparation for the jump. In a well-executed jump the right (free) leg reaches low and straight behind the skater with the body weight over the left foot (figure 8.24). The back should be straight but slightly inclined forward with the shoulders level. The left arm should be in front over the print and the right arm behind. The left foot draws toward the right, with the weight kept over the right foot for the takeoff. Both arms pull down, then up and in toward the body. The most common error is changing from a back outside edge to a back inside just before takeoff. If this occurs then the jump becomes a flip instead of a Lutz.

Figure 8.24 The Lutz jump takes off from a left back outside edge, placing the right toe into the ice.

TAKEOFF AND ROTATION

In the air the right leg should be straight and the left leg crossed slightly over in front of the right, with the left hip slightly lifted and the body weight remaining over the right side. The arms should be close to the body at chest level. One full revolution is turned, and then the left knee lifts slightly to uncross and the arms open before landing.

LANDING

The right back outside edge is used for the landing.

Do back crossovers and then hold the left back outside edge for the takeoff. Place the right toe into the ice and jump straight up without rotating. The purpose of this exercise is to practice remaining on the outside edge without changing over to the inside edge.

Combination Jumps

A **jump combination** links two jumps together by using the landing foot of the first jump as the takeoff for the second jump. A **jump sequence** is three or more jumps linked together. A combination is not legal if a turn or change of foot occurs between the jumps. The second jump of the combination is most commonly either a loop or a toe loop jump. The following jump combinations are common:

waltz/loop	waltz/toe loop
Salchow/loop	Salchow/toe loop
loop/loop	loop/toe loop
flip/loop	flip/toe loop
Lutz/loop	Lutz/toe loop
Axel/loop	Axel/toe loop

Occasionally a Salchow can be used as the second jump in a combination when the first jump is one that lands on a back inside edge, such as a one-footed Axel.

Problems occur in combination jumps when the first jump is poorly executed or when there is insufficient speed or poor timing between the first jump and the second. The first jump must have a controlled landing with a strong checked position for the second jump to be executed securely. Another common mistake is for the first jump to be strong and high and the second jump to be weak and small. To be of good quality, both jumps should be equal. Each should be high and well positioned and should have a strong, secure landing. To have enough spring into the second jump, the knee must not bend too deeply on the landing of the first jump.

Training Tip

With all combination jumps, make sure you can execute each jump of the combination with sureness and consistency. When troubles occur in the combination, go back to practicing the single jumps separately. Much of the success in combination jumps comes from good body positions and strength resulting from off-ice conditioning.

Multi-Rotational Jumps

The most common multi-rotational jumps are the Salchow, toe loop, loop, flip, Lutz, and Axel, and they are usually learned in that order. This section also discusses the double toe Walley. Once again, the instructions apply to skaters who rotate to the left, or counterclockwise. Skaters who rotate to the right will simply need to reverse the starting foot and direction.

Before moving on to the detailed descriptions of each jump, however, it will be helpful to know some of the basic principles that govern jumping and rotating. The following explanation will help you understand the mechanics behind multi-rotational jumps.

Jumping Theory

The biomechanics of jumping has been explored rather thoroughly in the last few years and continues to be the subject of numerous studies. All agree on a few basic premises. The height and length of a jump are proportional to the vertical and horizontal forces generated at takeoff. If the horizontal force (speed) is much greater than the vertical thrust (the energy of the arms, knee, ankle, and free leg), then the jump will be very long and not very high. If, however, the vertical thrust is greater than the horizontal, then the jump will be high and not very long. Proper integration of these forces at takeoff is important to ensure that the energy of the jump is not prematurely dissipated or inefficiently applied. For example, the lower and upper body must maintain the same vertical axis. Failure to maintain the correct vertical axis occurs when the free shoulder is ahead of the skating shoulder at takeoff, causing the jump to be overrotated at landing.

The sport science and technology division of the United States Olympic Committee (USOC) conducted a 1992 study in which triple Axels were videotaped, transferred to a computer, and digitized, thereby enabling the creation of three-dimensional representations of each jump. This study has given coaches a better understanding of the basic physics that govern jumping and rotating. The biomechanical analysis done by Dr. Sarah Smith and Dr. Debbie King led to the conclusion that two of the most important elements in figure skating jumps are rotational speed and flight time. These studies have been continued over the past several years with work done on the triple toe loop, triple Lutz, triple flip, and quad jumps.

In a multi-rotational jump, a skater exerts force against the ice to initiate rotation. Once the skater is in the air, however, there are no significant forces to change the angular momentum, which equals the skater's moment of inertia (resistance to rotation) multiplied by the angular velocity (rotational speed). Therefore skaters must generate angular momentum for triple or quadruple jumps before leaving the ice. The moment of inertia depends on body position and is greater when a skater is in an open position than when in a closed position. The farther the limbs are from the axis of rotation, the slower the rotation.

Although a skater's angular momentum cannot be changed during flight, resistance to rotation and speed of rotation can be changed. When the body position becomes more open, speed of rotation decreases. Conversely, when the body position is more closed, speed of rotation increases. During flight, skaters increase their rotational speeds by pulling in tightly. Skaters open up the body position to decrease the rotational speed when landing jumps.

The angular momentum appears to be increased on the triple Axel by the following methods:

- Decreasing the height of the arms and free leg
- Stepping the takeoff leg over more quickly
- Increasing the skid length and width

To further explain the theory of skids on takeoffs, World and Olympic coach Don Laws has defined three types of skids: increasing, diminishing (or decreasing), and controlled (or constant). The increasing skid is the most serious error resulting in a poor jump and the controlled skid is the most acceptable. It is rare to see a diminishing skid, but it may occur on a double Axel once the triple Axel has been mastered. The old theory was that there should be no skid at all, but that has given way to the realism that controlled skids are a necessary element to the forward takeoff edge of Axels.

In analyzing the relationship between the speed of a jump and its distance and duration, the study found that skaters attained similar heights and spent about the same time in the air for single, double, and triple Axels. The skaters traveled farther in their single Axels than in their double Axels, and the shortest distance occurred in the triple Axel.

In summary, the following theories were reinforced:

- Angular momentum (or rotational force) is determined by both body position and rotational speed and does not change once the skater leaves the ice.
- The skater must generate as much angular momentum as possible during takeoff for a multi-rotational jump.*
- Once in the air, a skater controls speed of rotation by closing or opening the body position.
- Skaters achieve the tightest position as quickly as possible by lifting their arms less and raising the knee of the free leg less in the triple Axel than in the single or double Axel.

Although not every skater or coach will have the opportunity to execute or teach a triple Axel, many of the concepts are the same in any multi-rotational jump.

Double Salchow

The double Salchow begins from a left back inside edge, jumping into the air and rotating two full revolutions before landing on a right back outside edge.

PREPARATION

The most common entry to the double Salchow is the same as the entry to a single Salchow: a left forward outside three. The checked position after the three is

---

*Note: This statement has been met with some controversy. Although the research done by USOC biochemists found it to be true, many coaches do not agree with this theory.

extremely important to establish control and set up the rotation for the jump. The left arm should be in front of the body and the right arm behind. The body weight stays over the left (skating) foot.

TAKEOFF AND ROTATION

All of the instructions previously given for the single Salchow apply, but the actions are quicker and tighter. The jump begins with a deep knee bend just before the right (free) arm and the right (free) foot come forward in a circular pattern past the skating foot and into the takeoff. Pressure is maintained on the front of the blade with increased pressure on the foot and ankle against the ice. The shoulders and hips stay level; they must not drop too far over to the back inside takeoff edge. Rotation is created as the hips come around to face the direction of travel and as the right foot lifts up. The left knee straightens and the right side rotates into the back scratch position with the left foot crossed in front over the right at the mid-calf level. The arms pull in across the chest with the elbows pointing down. Two full turns are rotated in the air.

LANDING

Just before landing, the left leg uncrosses, lifts, and then stretches back in an explosive action. The jump lands on a well-bent knee on the right back outside edge in a strong landing position.

Practice stepping into a back scratch spin from a left back inside three and then stepping forward into a right forward inside three and into the back scratch, emphasizing the change of weight from left to right.

Training Tip

The air position in all multi-rotational jumps is the same:

- One half rotation occurs at the apex of the jump.
- The body weight shifts from the takeoff to the landing side.
- The arms pull in across the center of the chest with the elbows down.
- The free leg is crossed in front of the skating leg, slightly above the ankle, with the free hip raised slightly higher than the skating hip.
- The head is slightly rotated toward the direction of flight.

Triple Salchow

The preparation, takeoff, rotation, and landing are the same for the triple Salchow as for the double, but the actions are even quicker and tighter. As the rotation increases, so must the strength, power, tightness of positions, and quick reflexes (or fast-twitch muscles). With the increased forces going into the triple Salchow, there is a greater chance to tilt the body too far into the curve of the takeoff edge. It is important to be in control of the speed going into the jump and to fully transfer the weight on the takeoff from the left side to the right side to complete one and one-half rotations by the time the apex of the jump is reached and still have the strength and control to complete the remaining rotations on the descent. The jump lands on a deeply bent knee on a right back outside edge.

Upper body strength is important in all triple jumps. Work with off-ice exercises and free weights to develop the strength and power necessary for triple jumps. All off-ice training should be supervised by a trained professional. Areas to concentrate on are upper body strength, hamstrings, and quads. See chapter 3 for more advice on off-ice conditioning.

Double Toe Loop

The double toe loop takes off from a right back outside edge assisted by a toe tap from the left foot. It makes two full revolutions in the air before landing on a right back outside edge.

PREPARATION

The most common entry is from either a right forward inside three turn or a series of push threes. The back outside edge of the last turn is held, and the left toe is placed into the ice for the takeoff (figure 8.25a).

Another variation is to take off from a left forward outside three. After the turn, the right foot steps down on the back outside edge, and the left toe is placed in the ice for the takeoff.

a   b

Figure 8.25   Double toe loop: *(a)* Preparation, and *(b)* air position.

TAKEOFF AND ROTATION

All of the instructions previously given for the single toe loop apply, but the actions are quicker and tighter. In the ideal position, the skating knee is well bent and the free leg reaches low and straight while the left arm extends forward and the right arm back. The body weight is over the skating hip, the shoulders are level, and the hips are square to the tracing. The arms should draw down toward the body, then up and into the air position as the body begins to rotate and leave the ice. At the same time, the right foot pulls toward the left toe on the takeoff and continues to draw past it. The momentum of the leg action and the arms vaults the body into the air (figure 8.25b). Two full revolutions are turned before landing.

LANDING

The jump lands on the right back outside edge.

Practice the entrance on a straight line. Concentrate on the pulling action of the takeoff by placing the left toe in the ice and drawing the right foot beside the left. Watch the placement of the toe pick; if it's placed too far to the side it will cause a twisted, prematurely-rotated jump.

Also practice Axels using a sideways step/together/step takeoff from the toes.

Triple Toe Loop

All of the previous instructions for the single and double toe loops apply; the actions are simply quicker and tighter.

On all triple jumps, practice correct stationary positions to help memorize body placement and alignment. Biomechanical studies show that in order for a triple jump to be completed, it is necessary to be into the second rotation at the apex of the jump. Triples pull in sooner and stay in longer.

Double Toe Walley

Skaters rarely perform the double Walley, because it is a difficult jump and is often not recognized or appreciated by audiences or judges. A double toe Walley is more common. It is a Walley jump with the addition of a toe assist on the takeoff. From the right back inside edge, the left toe is placed in the ice, and the body lifts off and rotates two full turns in the air before landing on a right back outside edge. This jump is often confused with the double toe loop, which takes off from a back outside rather than a back inside edge.

PREPARATION

Two common methods are used. One is a chain of back inside/outside/inside changes of edge, with the last back inside edge held and extended just before the left toe is placed in the ice for the takeoff. The other is a left forward outside three followed by a step down on the right back inside edge for the takeoff. Both entries use a strong checked position with the left arm in front of the body and right arm behind. The left toe is placed in the ice and the right foot is drawn to the left using the same action as in a double toe loop. The only difference is that the jump takes off from a back inside rather than a back outside edge. The skating knee is bent.

TAKEOFF AND ROTATION

All of the previous instructions for the single toe Walley apply, but the actions are quicker and tighter. In the ideal position, the skating knee is well bent and the free leg reaches low and straight while the left arm extends forward and the right arm back. The body weight is over the skating hip, the shoulders are level, and the hips are square to the tracing. The arms should draw down toward the body and then pass close by the body and lift up together in the air as the body begins to rotate and leave the ice. At the same time, the right foot pulls toward the left toe on the takeoff and continues to draw past it. The momentum of the legs and arms vaults the body into the air for two full revolutions before the landing.

LANDING

The landing takes place on the right back outside edge.

To feel the action of the takeoff, practice jumping from the right back inside edge to the left back inside edge without rotation. Remember to remain on the back inside edge at all times.

Double Loop

The double loop jump begins from a right back outside edge, jumping into the air and rotating two full revolutions before landing on the same edge as the takeoff—the right back outside.

PREPARATION

Entry commonly begins from a left forward outside three, stepping down onto the right back outside edge for the takeoff. An alternate entry is a series of back outside threes with a pump step between each, then a final three that lifts off into the double loop. The momentum of the edge on entering the double loop initiates the rotation. The thighs stay close together and the free foot remains over the print for the takeoff. The left arm must remain tightly checked in front of the body; the right arm stays behind. If the arm position is released before takeoff, many errors can occur, including little or no liftoff, insufficient rotation, and body imbalance.

TAKEOFF AND ROTATION

All of the previous instructions for the single loop apply, but the action is quicker and tighter. As the body lifts into the air, the arms pull up and in. The air position is tighter and the left (free) leg position is crossed in front of the right a little lower than on a single loop.

LANDING

On landing the jump, all rotation must be completed before the blade hits the ice. The checked position is a little more explosive than on the single loop, and the knee bend is greater to ensure a soft landing.

Practice multiple single loop combination jumps one after the other. Do the same with back scratch spins.

Triple Loop

The first triple loop was completed by Richard Button in 1952. Its execution is similar to that of the single and double loops. The significant difference for the triple is quicker timing and tighter positions.

A study done by biomechanics researchers at the Olympic Training Center (OTC) indicates that there is little difference in the actual time spent in the air during single, double, and triple jumps. This means that strength, speed, and quick reflexes must be increased to add more rotations in the same amount of time. The air position on a triple is very tight, with the arms held closer to the body than on a double loop and the free leg nearly straight but still crossed at the ankle.

Biomechanical research on triple jumps has also shown that upper body strength plays as important a role as the strength and power generated from the legs. The arms must be able to pull in quickly and match the explosive force of the legs on the takeoff. Quicker reflexes, increased strength, and a tighter air position help to create the dynamics necessary to increase rotation from a double to a triple. Shoulders and hips must remain level and parallel to the ice surface.

On landing the jump, all rotation must be completed before the blade hits the ice. The landing is more explosive and powerful than on the double loop, and the knee bend must be greater to absorb the force of the landing. A strong check is required to control rotation and balance on the landing.

A good on-ice exercise for the triple loop is a double loop/double loop combination jump. This helps to teach quickness and tightness.

Double Flip

The double flip jump is executed by skating on a left back inside edge and placing the right toe into the ice before lifting off and rotating two full turns, then landing on a right back outside edge.

PREPARATION

Either a left forward outside three or a right forward inside Mohawk can be executed in preparation for the jump. The turn must not swing wide but rather be performed closer to a straight line. The length of the edge going into the turn should match the length of the edge after the turn before the takeoff. In a well-executed double flip, the right (free) leg reaches low and straight behind the skater with the body weight over the left (skating) foot (figure 8.26a). The back should be straight but slightly inclined forward with the shoulders level. The left arm should be in front of the body over the print, and the right arm should be behind. The left (skating) knee should be well bent.

TAKEOFF AND ROTATION

All previous instructions for the single flip apply to the double flip. The left foot is drawn toward the right, transferring the weight to the right foot for the takeoff.

The right foot executes a strong push off (or vaulting action). Both arms pull down and then up and in toward the body. In the air, the right leg is straight and the left leg is crossed slightly over in front of the right (figure 8.26b). The hips are tilted so that the left hip is slightly raised over the right, causing the body weight to be balanced over the right side. The arms should be centered across the chest with the elbows down. After two full revolutions have been turned, the left leg lifts slightly to uncross and the arms open before landing.

LANDING

The jump lands on the right back outside edge.

Stand on the floor on two feet. Jump up and turn two revolutions, landing again on two feet. Draw the arms in on the rotation and out for the landing. Make sure a spotter is close by until your balance is secure.

a   b

Figure 8.26   Double flip: *(a)* Preparation, and *(b)* air position.

Triple Flip

All previous instructions for the single and double flips apply to the triple flip, but the actions must be quicker and tighter.

Double Lutz

The double Lutz jump is exactly like the double flip except that the takeoff edge is a back outside instead of a back inside edge. The double Lutz is executed by skating on a left back outside edge, placing the right toe into the ice, lifting off, and rotating two full turns before landing on a right back outside edge.

PREPARATION

The double Lutz is most commonly entered by doing back crossovers and then holding the left back outside edge in preparation for the jump. In a well-executed double Lutz, the right (free) leg reaches low and straight behind the skater with the body weight over the left foot. The back should be straight but slightly inclined forward with the shoulders level. The left arm should be in front over the print and the right arm should be behind. The left foot draws toward the right, and the weight remains over the right foot for the takeoff. Both arms pull down and then up and in toward the body. The most common error is changing from a back outside to a back inside edge just before takeoff. If this occurs then the jump becomes a double flip instead of a double Lutz, commonly known as a "flutz."

TAKEOFF AND ROTATION

All previous instructions for the single Lutz apply to the double Lutz. In the air, the right leg is straight and the left leg is crossed slightly over in front of the right. The hips are tilted so that the left hip is slightly raised over the right, causing the body weight to be balanced over the right side. The arms should be centered across the chest with the elbows down. After two full revolutions have been turned, the left leg lifts slightly to uncross and the arms open before landing.

LANDING

The landing is on the right back outside edge.

Training Tip

If a change of edge occurs on the takeoff, go back to practicing the takeoff in a single Lutz.

Triple Lutz

All previous instructions for the single and double Lutz apply to the triple Lutz. As with the single and double Lutz, the most common error is changing from a back outside edge to a back inside just before takeoff.

Master the Move

Brian Boitano's Picture-Perfect Jumps

Photo courtesy of Leah Adams

The air position in Boitano's jumps is textbook perfect—straight from head to toes, with square hips and shoulders, and tight arms and legs.

Brian Boitano's jumping technique is the standard by which to judge and critique jumps. His jumps are nearly textbook perfect.

Boitano has not only perfected his jumping technique but he also has created new variations of some of the standard jumps. The "Tano" is a triple Lutz executed with one arm raised above the head while the other rests on the waist. The Lutz is difficult enough without this dramatic arm position, which has become a trademark for the 1988 Olympic champion.

With so much emphasis placed on jumping—and now with quads and even quints on the horizon—it is especially important for a skater to nail the techniques and to distinguish oneself from the crowd. This can be achieved this through hard work, discipline, and innovation.

Double Axel

The double Axel starts with the left forward outside edge, rotates two and one-half turns in the air, and lands on the right back outside edge.

PREPARATION

All of the entry alternatives discussed for the single Axel on page 152 can be used for the double Axel as well. The most common preparation is a left forward outside three turn ending with a step back on a right back outside edge and then a step forward on the left outside edge.

TAKEOFF AND ROTATION

All previous instructions for the single Axel apply to the double Axel. The left (skating) knee is well bent with the right (free) foot extended to the back. As in the single Axel, the free leg must swing forward in a straight line and not around on the takeoff, though the knee of the free leg is bent. There will be a skid or scrape on the takeoff edge. This is expected but should be kept to a minimum. If there is too much rotation before the jump leaves the ice, the rotation needs to be reduced. Reducing the rotation will in turn reduce an excessive skid on the takeoff.

Because the double Axel is really two and one-half turns in the air, it is the transition jump into triples. An important skill to master is the weight shift from the left side to the right into the loop or back spin position, which should occur at the beginning of the jump. At the apex nearly one half of the rotation must be completed in order to finish and correctly land the completed jump. The body position must be tight in the air with the shoulders, arms, and hips level. The arms should pull in across the center of the chest with the elbows down. The left leg should be crossed in front, slightly above the ankle, with the left hip slightly lifted. The position of the head is optional. It can either be slightly rotated toward the left or remain straight ahead. The upper body must remain erect and firm throughout the entire jump.

LANDING

For the landing, the left knee lifts slightly up and then passes in a straight line close by the right (landing) leg. The arms open up and break out, pushing back to a checked landing position. The right (landing) knee is well bent and the left (free) leg is extended fully behind. Upper body strength is important. The back must remain straight, the shoulders level, and the body weight balanced over the right foot.

A good practice jump is the waltz/double loop combination. A fast back scratch spin with a strong exit helps to strengthen the air position and landing action. You can also do several double loop jumps in a row to feel the tighter body position. Another common exercise is a double bell jump (explained in the single Axel exercises on page 154) executed with a two-footed landing. The purpose of this exercise is to feel body and air positions without having to concentrate on the landing.

Triple Axel

All previous instructions for the single and double Axels apply to the triple Axel. As the rotation increases, so must the strength, power, tightness of positions, and quick reflexes. With the increased forces going into the triple Axel, there is a greater chance to tilt the body or have the body weight unbalanced—usually too far back. It is important to be in control of the speed going into the jump and to fully transfer the weight on the takeoff from the left side to the right side to complete half the rotation upon reaching the apex of the jump and still have the strength and control to complete the other half during the descent. The jump lands on a well bent knee on a right back outside edge.

Quads

Detailed descriptions of the quad jumps are not necessary: the basic instructions for the corresponding double and triple apply to each quad. As rotation increases, the same elements are essential:

- Tighter, more streamlined positions
- Quicker reflexes
- Increased strength
- Greater power and speed

Off-ice conditioning and strength training are mandatory. The quads, hamstrings, glutes, abdominals, and upper body muscles must be trained for strength and quickness.

Tools for Learning Jumps

The following tools are useful for teaching and learning jumps. They can help beginning skaters feel more comfortable when first learning jumps, and they can help more advanced skaters refine and perfect their jumps.

- **Harness**—A harness is an invaluable aid in introducing Axels and double and triple jumps. This tool, properly used, helps skaters develop timing, muscle memory in performing and landing a jump, and increased confidence. Remember, it is only a tool. If you do not have a harness installed at your rink, a hand-held harness is useful. If you're a coach and you've never used a harness, be sure to ask another coach for assistance before putting a student on the harness.

- **Impact Pads**—Impact pads protect skaters against injury when falling repeatedly on jumps. Although skaters find these pads too cumbersome to use all the time, they are often an aid when learning a jump.

- **Video Camera**—Videotaping jumps is another wonderful learning and teaching aid. Some rinks provide a rink-side video camera. During freestyle sessions a coach or other designated person is available to tape skaters on request. The skater can perform a jump and immediately view it on the screen. The coach should review jumps with the skater to point out strengths and weaknesses.

The OTC Elite Training Camp uses a highly sophisticated form of videotaping to analyze elite skaters' jumps. The biomechanical variables computed include free leg position, takeoff angle, vertical and horizontal velocity, rotational velocity, time to attain the rotating position, and jump height. The skater, assisted by a coach, is then able to evaluate each jump on the following five criteria:

1. Preparation or setup
2. Takeoff
3. Air position
4. Landing
5. Speed

Although these sophisticated cameras are not available to all skaters, coaches can view video performances with these check points in mind.

Don Laws, coach of Olympic champion Scott Hamilton, suggests looking for six common jumping errors:

1. Excessive lean in the airborne position
2. Imbalanced ratio of jump height to jump distance
3. Pounding of toe in toe jump takeoff
4. Excessive curve of edge at takeoff
5. Pelvic area off the line of balance
6. Lack of rhythmic process

He also identifies six qualities to look for:

1. Speed
2. Height
3. Distance
4. Posture
5. Stability
6. Consistency

• **Off-Ice Training**—Off-ice jumping is extremely helpful for teaching and perfecting jumps in a nonthreatening environment. Off-ice conditioning is clearly a necessity if a skater is to achieve maximum potential in jumping. It's also a great protector against injury.

Summary

While you will employ many different techniques as you progress to increasingly difficult jumps, it is important to remember the basics. Speed, timing, and rhythm are necessities; consistent approaches and setup are also key factors. Successful jumps rely on strong, correct execution at three critical junctures: takeoff, air position, and landing.

It is important to keep jumps in perspective. They may be the most exciting element in a program, but not all skaters are gifted jumpers. Judges constantly encourage skaters not to overload a program with elements that cannot be executed effectively. They continue to stress that a high, strong, single jump is better than a small double jump that is cheated and barely leaves the ground.

chapter 9
Pairs

Pair skating is arguably the most exciting and dynamic discipline in skating. Teams like Randy and Tai, JoJo and Ken, and the Carruthers have made audiences sit on the edge of their seats, holding their breath before the landing of a throw or gasping in disbelief when a triple twist gets tossed high into the air. Pair skating requires the strength of both partners along with their technical ability and perfect unison.

Of primary importance to a good pair team is their physical appearance. Body types must be similar. The man should be at least a head taller than the lady (although there are exceptions, like the Kauffmans: Ron was easily a foot taller than Cindy). The team must also be compatible and able to resolve the differences that will undoubtedly surface, sometimes on a daily basis. Such conflicts include physical, psychological, and emotional differences.

A good coach counsels the partners to support one another, not laying blame for mistakes but analyzing problems and working together to find solutions. Just as in any good partnership, it is important to determine each team member's strengths and use them to cover each other's weaknesses.

Pair partners are seldom from the same family and often do not reside in the same city. Therefore decisions must be made about who moves, where will the pair train, who will be the coach, and how expenses will be shared. Support is needed from both families. When there is mutual respect and commitment, the effort is doubly rewarding.

In addition to traditional pair teams, there are also *similar pairs,* where two men or two ladies skate with each other. Similar pairs are often seen in ice shows or in recreational skating. This is a good alternative when there is a shortage of male skaters or when a club or community ice show wants to add variety and interest. In the 50s and 60s the Ice Follies made a tradition of featuring twin sisters performing together in routines that delighted the audiences. Popular twin acts were the Scotvolds, the Pastors, the Thomases, and the Perkys. The Follies and other touring ice shows also highlighted male skaters performing together; the most notable were the Schramms, who skated while chained to each other. Pair skating is fun and innovative!

Safety

Training in a safe environment is always important but especially so with pair teams. Of primary consideration is the understanding and strength necessary to execute each maneuver. Each member of the team must have complete confidence in the other. Pair teams must schedule regular off-ice practices and develop strong off-ice conditioning programs. When learning a new and difficult skill, the pair must practice it over and over off the ice until competence is attained and each partner is comfortable with the other. An authorized spotter must supervise, and the coach must certify that the skill is ready before the skaters take it to the ice. Some teams practice lifts in a swimming pool, which makes for a much softer landing than the floor or the ice.

On the ice, it is necessary to limit the number of pair teams practicing at one time; ideally, there should be no more than four senior level teams or six to eight preliminary teams. Caution should be exercised when mixing levels of teams during

---

This chapter was reviewed and edited by Jay Freeman. Freeman was a national and international pairs competitor. He toured professionally with Torvill and Dean and has been a coach and chairman for the National Pair Tryouts. He holds a master rating in pairs and a senior rating in freestyle.

the same practice session. Pair teams and single skaters should not occupy the same practice session if this situation can be avoided.

Although serious accidents rarely occur on the ice, it is always wise to be prepared. All coaches should practice first aid sport safety and CPR skills. A first aid kit and emergency phone numbers should be easily accessible, and skaters should never be allowed to practice alone in a rink.

In recent years the discussion of helmets has been met with varying opinions. For young tots the wearing of helmets is a good practice. With pair teams there are mixed views. In the few cases where serious accidents have occurred, it has been established that a helmet would not have prevented a skull injury. There is also concern that helmets limit vision and add bulk that might contribute to an accident. Lastly, there is apprehension that if helmets are required in practice, then they should also be required in competition. Interestingly, none of the serious accidents that have occurred happened on a new or particularly difficult skill; each was rather the result of poor ice conditions, fatigue, or a previously weakened condition. In these cases, the accidents might have been avoided if close attention had been paid to these contributing factors.

Basic Techniques

For the sake of clarity, all instructions in this chapter will be directed to the man or the lady and will assume both skaters jump in a counterclockwise direction.

Stroking

Aligning two bodies to move as one and developing unity in style and timing is the ultimate goal of a pair team. This is addressed from the first lesson to the last. Even though basic skills become second nature, each new skill or combination of skills must be learned and then practiced over and over again to perfect timing and unison.

All skaters must have a preliminary level of competence in moving across the ice before pair skating can be attempted, but even those as young as six or seven years of age can experience the fun of skating with a partner. A simple beginning is side-by-side forward stroking. This skill is begun at a standstill, with the partners standing beside each other and holding hands. For young skaters even the simple act of holding hands can be traumatic and uncomfortable. Coaches need to be patient and sensitive to these feelings.

Begin by starting with the same foot. Work on matching the push off, the length of the stroke, and the timing of the change from one foot to another. (See figure 9.1.) At first there will be a little tug and pull as each partner learns to adjust to the other. When the timing begins to match, so does the exhilaration and fun of performing even a simple skill together.

Next, begin again from a standstill but change the hand positions. Each partner's hands should be raised to the other's shoulder as the pair begins forward stroking. This hand position is a little more difficult as it does not allow the partners as much freedom to deviate from one another; thus it becomes an exercise as well as a varied position.

The third hand position that can be introduced to new pair skaters is the pair position. The lady begins on the man's right side. The palm of her left hand should be placed into the palm of his left hand and stretched across his chest. Her elbow must remain in a locked position. The man's right arm is placed behind the lady and

Figure 9.1 Side-by-side forward stroking.

Figure 9.2 Forward crossovers.

on her right hip. Her right arm is extended out to her right side as would be standard for a forward stroking position. At first, this position is very awkward because of the close proximity of the two skaters, but with practice it proves to be the most basic and practical of all pair hand positions. With this placement of arms and bodies, the man can help to control unison and direction. When speed is gained and corners are rounded, the lady should be slightly ahead of the man, and as skills are mastered, she may add varied arm positions with her free arm to accent the mood, music, or interpretation of the program.

Forward Crossovers

When the pair rounds the corners of the rink in forward stroking, forward crossovers are executed (figure 9.2). The pair position remains unchanged except that the man presses the lady slightly forward so that she leads and he follows. The push off, stroke, and crossover should match precisely every step of the way. Even the head positions—looking forward, to the side, up, or down—should match. So must the bend of the skating knee and the extension of the free foot. A team that is well matched and in perfect unison begins to move as one unit instead of two.

Back Crossovers

With the partners standing side by side and using the hand-to-hand position, begin back crossovers in a clockwise or a counterclockwise direction with the man leading and the lady following (figure 9.3). Although back crossovers would rarely, if ever, start from a standstill position, it is a good place to begin with a new team. To gain speed by starting backward is very difficult; therefore the purpose of this exercise is not speed but the timing and unison necessary to do back crossovers together.

Once this skill is understood, return to a side-by-side starting position. Each partner should turn a forward outside three, then grasp the other's hands and begin the back crossovers. This skill should also be practiced in the shoulder-to-shoulder position and, as with all crossovers, should be practiced in both the clockwise and counterclockwise directions.

Figure 9.3 Back crossovers.

Combining Stroking and Crossovers

When forward stroking, forward crossovers, and back crossovers have been confidently performed, the three skills can be added together. The team begins by stroking forward in a counterclockwise direction and doing forward crossovers around the end of the rink in pair position. As the forward crossovers are completed and the end of the rink is rounded, each partner should glide forward on two feet and, cutting through the center of the ice, the man takes the lead, slightly forward of the lady. The pair position changes to hand-to-hand, and then the team turns a right forward outside three and begins back crossovers. In choreographed programs there are instances when the lady leads and the man follows.

Side-by-Side Elements

As indicated earlier, a preliminary level of competence is required to begin a pair team. It is possible to start a team when the skaters are quite young and possess few skills. In this case each skater must continue to learn individual skills and then add them to the pair repertoire.

Often, singles skaters decide later in their training that they would like to try pair skating. These skaters may already have learned all of the basic and combination spins and the single, double, and triple jumps. Progress with skaters at this level is very rapid. It is also not uncommon for partners to change. The reasons are many. The skaters may be incompatible, they may have difficulty in traveling to train together, or the lady may begin to outgrow the man. There are many examples of accomplished teams who have changed partners and, because of their background and training, have easily been able to adapt their skills in a short time and make an impressive show at national competition.

When young and inexperienced skaters are paired, the progress is much slower. After basic hand positions, stroking, and crossovers have been learned, try side-by-side spins and jumps at the appropriate level. Every movement must be synchronized from the entrance of the maneuver to the exit.

Spins

In side-by-side pair spins, partners must perfectly synchronize every segment of the spins: the back crossovers or three-turn entry, the placement of the spins on the ice in relation to each other, the speed and number of rotations in the spin, and the timing of the exit. Even the rotations in the spin must be perfectly matched so that each partner is always facing the same direction at the same time, as shown in figure 9.4. How can all this be accomplished? It is a matter of timing, rhythm, and spotting. With much practice, it is a skill that can be perfected and consistent.

Unison begins at the entry of the spin, which must have identical entry steps. Each partner must be facing in the same direction. A specific count or cadence should be practiced every time, without variation. One skater is the designated spotter, following the lead of the other. At least one of the skaters must possess the ability to increase or decrease speed to stay matched with the other. When perfected, these combined skills become so polished that they are not recognized by the observer.

Teaching Tip

Have the skaters practice side-by-side spins using the concept of a clock. With an erasable magic marker, draw the faces of two clocks side by side on the ice, approximately eight to twelve feet apart, marking the quarter hours. Train the skaters to enter the clock at the same "time" (e.g., 6:00). Determine a "time," based on the abilities of the skaters, to bring the free leg around, draw in the arms, release the free leg, and exit. As the skaters become

Figure 9.4   Side-by-side camel spins.

more proficient, the clocks should be drawn closer and closer together until they are only a few feet apart. Eventually the skaters will be able to visualize the clocks without you drawing them on the ice, and they will have developed the precise timing needed for unison.

A good exercise is to practice timing and unison off the ice as well as on. Walk through the spin on the floor to understand exactly where each partner must be at a given time. Eliminating the flow and speed that naturally occur on the ice allows each skater time to think through every move of the spin.

Jumps

Unison is as important in side-by-side jumps as it is in spins. In the beginning skaters are separated by some distance, but as they become more proficient the space between them closes and the difficulty of the jump or jump combination increases. It is natural for a man to jump higher and cover more distance than a lady. This problem can be solved by correcting the disparity at the beginning of the jump. The lady can be positioned slightly ahead of the man and take off a split second after he does. The end result is that the partners land their jumps at the same time and in close proximity to each other, giving the impression of unity (figure 9.5).

It is possible to have partners that jump and spin in opposite directions. This disparity can be effectively choreographed in what is called mirror skating; the same principles, however, apply in producing precise timing and unison.

To develop bigger jumps that cover more distance, work off the ice with plyometrics, as explained in detail in Chapter 3.

Figure 9.5 Side-by-side jumps.

Pair Spins

In executing pair spins, both partners must spin in the same direction. If one spins opposite from the other, either one of the members of the team has to learn to spin in the other direction or both skaters need to find new partners.

A pair spin is entered from opposite sides of the same circle (figure 9.6a). The partners meet in the center of the circle (figure 9.6b) and assume the pair position, whether in a sit spin or camel (figure 9.6c). Many new and creative spins have been invented in the past 10 years. These new, untraditional spins require great flexibility and control. They have added a great deal of interest and excitement to pair spins.

Off-ice conditioning as discussed in chapter 3 and walk-throughs on the floor are helpful to establish positions and timing.

Lifts

One of the most exciting and challenging parts of pair skating is, of course, the lifts. This is where off-ice training becomes necessary and spotters mandatory. Even simple lifts with a new team can cause the man to become unbalanced, resulting in a hard fall on the floor or ice. Strength is particularly necessary for the man in the back, arms, and legs. For the lady it is especially important to have a strong back and strong arms. Off-ice training is essential, and practicing in front of a mirror is helpful.

Up-and-Down Lift

There are many types of lifts. The most basic are the straight up-and-down lift, which involves no rotation, and the waltz lift, which is just one half turn. In the up-and-down

a

b

c

Figure 9.6   Camel spin: *(a)* Partners start from opposite sides of the circle, then *(b)* meet in the center and *(c)* assume the pair position.

lift the lady stands in front of the man, both facing to the front. The man places his hands on the lady's waist and she places her hands on top of his (figure 9.7a). Both partners bend their knees at the same time. As the man lifts the lady upward, she uses the force of the floor at first, and the ice later, to push off and assist in the lift (figure 9.7b).

a   b

Figure 9.7 Up-and-down lift: *(a)* Both partners start facing to the front, then *(b)* the man lifts the lady upward.

Training Tip

The man must keep the lady close in front of him and lift her straight into the air. The lady must keep her body aligned over her feet and hold her back straight.

In the first few tries the object is not to obtain height but to get the feel of the jump and to develop timing. It is common for the lady to break at the waist and for the man to have little strength, resulting in a small or low lift. As confidence, understanding, and strength are gained, the lift can be increased until the man's arms are fully extended above his head and the lift is held in a sustained position for a period of 10 to 15 seconds. The lady may experiment with various leg positions, such as a stag or split.

Practice this, and all lifts, on the floor before executing them on the ice.

Master the Move

The Beauty and Unison of Ludmilla and Oleg Protopopov

© EMPICS/Scanpix

Their elegance and perfectionism helped Ludmilla and Oleg Protopopov win gold medals at the 1964 and 1968 Olympics.

In the history of world pair skating, perhaps the most memorable team is Ludmilla and Oleg Protopopov from Russia. They had a finished style that exuded grace, athletic ability, unison, and an unbelievable love for skating.

Their costumes and music were always carefully chosen to reflect a theme that matched their style and technique. Every detail was important to their total performance. Every move had a purpose and was conscientiously placed in just the right spot in their program. The Protopopovs would spend hours on just one move to ensure perfection and, as a result, their performances mesmerized audiences around the world.

A good foundation in jumps, spins, and footwork is vital to achieving a strong team. Once a strong foundation is in place, it will take countless hours of practice to develop unity in style and timing. Attention to detail, perfection in technique, and insistence that every move be meaningful and relevant to the entire program are all qualities of an extraordinary pairs team. The presence of those same qualities in the Protopopovs explains why they left such an indelible mark on the sport.

Waltz Lift

The waltz lift begins from a hip-to-hip position with the lady on the man's right side. His left hand holds the lady's right hand in front of him, and her left hand rests on his right shoulder (figure 9.8a). His right hand is placed under her left armpit and is used to assist with the lift. The lady steps forward on her left foot, and both partners bend their knees at the same time in preparation for the jump. As the man lifts the lady into the air, she does a waltz jump across in front of him (figure 9.8b) and lands on a right back outside edge. The man's job is to lift the lady straight into the air using his legs and arms. Her job is to press down on the his hand and shoulder to assist with the lift. As the lady pushes down, the man lifts upward. At full height the lady should lock her elbows to provide stability for the lift.

Break the waltz lift down into its three basic components—lift, waltz jump, and landing—and practice each separately before hooking them all together.

a   b

Figure 9.8 Waltz jump: *(a)* Starting position, and *(b)* position of each partner at the height of the lift.

Waist Loop Lift

The waist loop lift begins with both partners in the same starting position as the straight up-and-down lift, with the man's hands on the lady's waist and her hands pressing down on his (figure 9.9a). Moving backward, both partners bend their knees. The lady pushes down on the man's wrists and arches her back as she is lifted into the air and above the man's head (figure 9.9b). The man rotates one full turn on the ice. Keeping his feet (his base) closely together, he steps from backward to forward and then follows with a right forward inside Mohawk. As he places the lady back down on the ice, he pushes off on a right back outside edge to match the lady's landing edge.

When the man is lifting the lady in the air and turning, he must keep his feet close together and move with small but smooth Mohawk steps. This maneuver takes a lot of practice to do well, as the man must move across the ice with shallow edges and without any jerky or disruptive movement.

a   b

Figure 9.9   Waist loop lift: *(a)* Starting position, and *(b)* position at the height of the lift.

Practice the Mohawk steps over and over in a straight line before trying them with a partner. Wide stepping can result in a loss of balance that may cause the team to stumble and fall.

Training Tip

The man must never look up at the lady when he is lifting her. Looking up causes him to arch his back, which shifts the weight to the heels and results in loss of balance.

Flip, Lutz, and Axel Lifts

These lifts are executed with the same hand positions as the waltz lift. The lady's takeoff position for each jump is exactly like that of the single jump it corresponds to. For example, on a flip lift, the lady turns a left forward outside three, which places her face to face and to the side of the man. She places her right toe in the ice, and both partners bend their knees in preparation for the lift. The man lifts the lady straight into the air and turns one full turn, placing her back on the ice on a right back outside landing edge. The man steps forward from his Mohawk turns and finishes on a left forward outside edge, both partners still facing each other.

Training Tip

When learning new lifts, practice them off the ice first, breaking them down into their major components before hooking them back together as a unit and executing them on the ice.

Overhead or Lasso Lift

The overhead lift is also called the lasso lift because the action of the lift is similar to a lasso. It begins with the man and lady in a side-to-side position with the lady's right hand stretched over her head and placed in the man's right hand, which is over his head. The lady's left hand is placed in the man's right hand, which is down and to the side between them. (See figure 9.10a.) In this starting position the arms are actually crossed, so that on the liftoff the man pulls the lady across in front of him, into the air, and over to his left side. He then extends his arms straight over his head and supports the lady behind him in a hand-to-hand position (figure 9.10b).

As she is lifted into the air, the lady must maintain a slightly arched back and keep her arms locked to provide a stable support between her and the man. At the midpoint of the lift, the lady is positioned above the man's head and is held behind his back with her legs in a semi-split position. The man continues to swing the lady around to his right side and places her on the ice in the dismount, letting go of her left hand but still holding onto her right hand. It helps for the man to bend his knees to decrease the distance from the height of the jump to the ice. The lady is placed gently down on the ice on a right back outside landing edge.

Training Tip

This lift requires a great deal of strength and off-ice training before being tried on the ice. The lady must "step up" into the air, staying close to the man and avoiding the tendency to swing out and away from him. The man must get under the lady with a very deep knee bend as he brings her across and to his left side.

a   b

Figure 9.10   Lasso lift: *(a)* Starting position and *(b)* midpoint of the lift.

Figure 9.11   Tabletop lift.

Tabletop or Platter Lift

More advanced lifts, like the tabletop lift shown in figure 9.11, are extremely difficult and can be dangerous if not properly taught and supervised. The lady must hold strong positions and be fearless and trusting of her partner. Other advanced lifts include hand-to-hand press lifts, split and lateral twists, and numerous varieties of other lifts, including combinations where the lady changes positions in the air.

Split Twist

The split twist begins with the man and lady skating backward and the man leading. The man pulls the lady backward toward him with her back facing him. The lady is now standing on her left foot, and the man is on two feet with the lady between his feet. At this point the man places his hands on the lady's waist, and then the lady places her hands on the man's wrists. She then picks with her right toe, placing the toe close to her left foot and being careful to avoid kicking the man.

As the lady starts to rise from the ice, the man assists by lifting her into the air to his left side at approximately 45 degrees. As he lifts her to the top she begins splitting her legs and starts to push off from the man's wrists (figure 9.12a). The man releases the lady (figure 9.12b) and turns forward to catch her at her hips (figure 9.12c) as she turns one half turn and faces him. She lands on the right back outside edge and steps forward as in a typical split jump landing. The man also extends his arms out, holding the lady's right hand with his left and finishing on his left forward outside edge.

Training Tip

Practice this lift without doing the split position to establish positions and timing. When the lift feels comfortable, add the split position.

Lateral Twist

The lateral twist begins with the man and lady both skating backward, with the man leading. The man pulls the woman toward him, and she extends her left leg back toward the man's right side. (The takeoff is similar to a star or cartwheel lift). The man places his right hand on the lady's left hip, and his left hand takes the lady's right hand in a palm-to-palm hold.

a

b

c

Figure 9.12 Split twist: *(a)* The lift, *(b)* release, and *(c)* catch.

The lady then picks the ice with her left toe and begins the vault. She is assisted by the man, who pushes up with his right hand on her left hip. The man simultaneously moves his left hand (and the lady's right hand) toward her right hip. As the lift reaches about shoulder height, the lady starts driving her right foot toward the ceiling and chases it with her left foot, pushing off from the man and pulling her arms in toward her body (figure 9.13). The man then turns forward and catches her as he did in the twist lift.

The lady should practice a chasing cartwheel (chasing the left foot after the right) on the floor and duplicate the action of the aerial part of the lift on the floor. As always, the man needs to work on strengthening the upper body as explained in chapter 3.

The man sets the pattern going into a lift and the lady tracks him in perfect unison and syncopation. Pair skaters are extremely innovative. New lifts and other pair moves are continually being invented. This variety of lifts and positions is another reason pair skating is so exciting.

Figure 9.13 Lateral twist.

Throws

The throw is another spectacular move in pair skating. It was invented by renowned pair coach Ron Ludington. The first throw was an Axel. Since its invention, throws have increased to Salchows, toe loops, and loops, and they have increased rotation from singles to doubles and triples.

Throw Axel

The throw Axel begins with both the lady and the man skating backward on a left back inside edge. The lady's right hand is in the man's left. The man is leading and the lady trailing. He draws her toward him, and then both partners drop hands and step to the right back outside edge. The man turns a right back outside Mohawk, and the lady steps on her left forward outside edge, placing the partners hip to hip. The man then places his right hand and arm behind the lady's back, and the lady places her left hand on the man's right shoulder. Her right hand is placed in his left in preparation for the Axel (figure 9.14a). He is stabilized on both feet while she is on a left forward outside edge directed straight toward him. He assists her into the air for the takeoff. She rotates one and one-half revolutions in the air (figure 9.14b) and lands on a right back outside edge. The man finishes in a semi-lunge with his left leg slightly leading.

a   b

Figure 9.14   Throw Axel: *(a)* Preparation, and *(b)* air position.

Throw Loop

The throw loop begins with the lady skating backward on a right back outside edge in front of the man, who is also skating backward but has both feet on the ice on a curve matching the lady's. His left foot is slightly in front of the right, and he is holding the lady in a waist lift position (figure 9.15a). Both partners bend their knees and then rise up simultaneously for the liftoff. The man turns a back outside three while lifting the lady, who executes a one-revolution loop jump in the air (figure 9.15b) before landing on a right back outside edge. The man catches her at the waist and finishes forward by pushing with the right foot onto a left forward outside edge, pushing the lady away from him landing on a right back outside edge.

a   b

Figure 9.15   Throw loop: *(a)* Preparation, and *(b)* air position.

Throw Salchow

Entry into the throw Salchow begins with either a three turn or a Mohawk. Both skaters enter from a back inside edge, the man leading the lady. He holds onto her waist with his right hand and holds her left hand in his. (See figure 9.16a.) She may place her right hand on top of his (optional). Her left arm is extended out for leverage on the takeoff. Before liftoff, the lady frees her right arm to assist in the takeoff. From the left back inside edge the lady is thrown into the air in a Salchow jump (figure 9.16b). She uses her left arm to help the man as he lifts her with his left hand and guides her into the air with his right. She lands on the right back outside edge, while the man rotates one half turn to finish forward in a semi-lunge with his left leg slightly leading his right.

Death Spirals

There are four types of death spirals, named for the edge on which the lady is skating—forward outside, forward inside, back outside, or back inside. The man is always in a pivot position, holding onto the lady's right hand with his right hand and extending his left hand either out to the side or above his head. He must pull away from the lady and keep his arm very stiff to provide firm tension between the partners. The rules state that the man must complete one full revolution with his partner.

Figure 9.16   Throw Salchow: *(a)* Preparation, and *(b)* air position.

The lady's job is to keep her body stable and solid. Her goal is to lower her head as close to the ice as possible without touching the ice. She must also avoid touching the ice with her free hand. Death spirals begin off the ice with the lady doing exercises to strengthen her back.

There is a choice of grips that may be used. In the *pinky grip* (figure 9.17a) the partners lock palms by gripping the man's pinky and the lady's thumb. In the *wrist grip* each partner grips the other's hand around the wrist. The lady may choose to keep her fingers together (figure 9.17b) or extend her index finger higher up on the man's wrist (figure 9.17c).

Forward Outside Death Spiral

The lady begins on a left forward outside edge, pushing her boot out away from the circle. Her right leg is tucked in front of the left with the thighs closed at the knees. She supports herself with her left hand pushing down against the man's right hand as he pushes up against her hand.

While the lady is supported by the hand or wrist, she pushes up toward the ceiling with her right hip higher than the left. As she is being lowered, her hips rotate clockwise toward the ceiling so that both hips are now facing the ceiling in the bridge position. The lady's head begins by looking forward and then rotates out and back toward the right shoulder. As the death spiral starts to lose tension from centrifugal force, the man pulls upward on the lady's hand. The lady lifts her head up and pulls

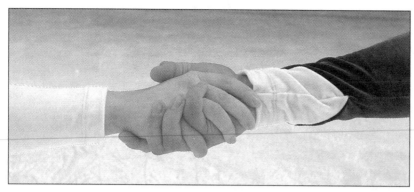

a

b

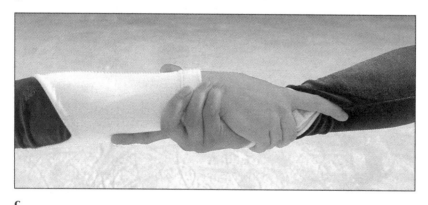

c

Figure 9.17 Death spiral grips: (a) Pinky grip, (b) wrist grip with fingers together, and (c) wrist grip with index finger extended.

her skating foot back under her hip. She exits the death spiral on the forward outside edge with her free leg extended behind her.

The man starts the death spiral from back crossovers. He turns outward to the circle, extending his left leg behind him and holding the lady up with his right hand. As he lowers her, he leans back slightly on the circle, keeping his right hand extended out of the circle and slightly behind him. His circle tightens as he lowers her, creating continuous tension to support the lady's bridge position. As this occurs his free leg starts to come behind him, and he places his toe pick in the ice in a back outside pivot. He draws his legs together until his right foot is right against but not touching his left foot. With his weight on his left foot, he extends his right arm out and pushes his partner away. The man finishes forward on the left foot with the lady forward in front of him.

Training Tip

The man's position and steps are the same for all four death spirals.

Forward Inside Death Spiral

The lady begins on a right forward inside edge, pushing her boot out away from the circle. Her left leg is tucked in front of the right, forming an open position. She supports herself with her left hand pushing down against the man's right hand as he pushes up against her hand.

While the lady is supported by the hand or wrist, she pushes up toward the ceiling with her right hip higher than the left. As she is being lowered, her hips rotate clockwise toward the ceiling so that both hips are now facing the ceiling in the bridge position. See figure 9.18. The lady's head begins by looking forward and then rotates out and back toward the right shoulder. As the death spiral starts to lose tension from centrifugal force, the man pulls upward on the lady's hand. The lady lifts her head up and pulls her skating foot back under her hip. She exits on the forward outside edge with her free leg extended behind her.

Figure 9.18   Forward inside death spiral.

Backward Inside Death Spiral

The lady begins on a left back inside edge, pushing her boot out away from the circle. Her right leg is in front of the left, and her knee is turned down toward the ice. She supports herself with her right hand pushing down against the man's right hand as he pushes up against her hand. She pushes her hips up toward the ceiling with her left hip on top. As she is being lowered, the hips stay vertical to the ice. Her head faces in toward her right arm, looking up at the man. As the death spiral hit its final bridge position, her head faces up toward the ceiling. As the death spiral starts to lose tension through centrifugal force, the man pulls upward on the lady's hand. The lady brings her head back up and pulls her skating foot back under her hip. She exits forward, turning a left inside bracket with her right free leg extended behind her.

Backward Outside Death Spiral

The lady begins on a right back outside edge, pushing her boot out away from the circle. Her left leg is in front of the right with the thighs closed at the knees. She supports herself with her right hand pushing down against the man's as he pushes up against her hand. As she is being supported by the hand or wrist, she pushes her hips up toward the ceiling with the left hip on top. The hips rotate counterclockwise toward the ceiling as she is being lowered, so that both hips are now facing the ceiling in a bridge position. See figure 9.19. The lady's head looks forward at the beginning of the death spiral and then rotates out and back toward the left shoulder. As the death spiral starts to lose tension through centrifugal force, the man pulls upward

Figure 9.19   Backward outside death spiral.

on the lady's hand. She brings her head up and pulls her skating foot back under her hip. She exits on a right back outside edge in front of her partner, with her left (free) leg extended behind her.

Summary

Pair skating is exciting, challenging, and demanding. A good foundation in basic jumps, spins, and footwork will pay off well for a team that wishes to advance to higher levels of competition. Even skaters who never plan to test or compete in pair skating should try this discipline to gain knowledge and to experience the sheer joy (or the absolute fear) of performing jumps, spins, and lifts with a partner.

part III
Performances

chapter 10
Program Elements and Choreography

Learning individual skating skills is similar to building a foundation for a house. A solid base is necessary in order to build something worthwhile. After you've laid the skating foundation, you can combine several skills together to create a skating program for freestyle, pairs, or dance. When a program that challenges a skater's strength and endurance is combined with a selection of music that captivates the spirit, mind and body soar as the skater moves from one end of the rink to the other. A program is a showpiece of technical skills and creative efforts.

A skater's first program may be only one minute long and combine only a few skills, but it is exhilarating, even if there is no audience. Skaters may wish to test, compete, skate in ice shows or exhibitions, or perform for an audience of one for their own personal satisfaction—but whatever the choice, there is nothing like the joy of skating to a personal program.

Music

Test and competitive skaters need to have the music they select edited and cut to include just the right tempos and meet the required length of time. In most cases coaches prepare the music for their skaters, but as skaters progress they may want to take a more active role or, at the very least, supervise the process. Each skater and coach needs to build a library of music and stay current with many types of music, from classical to jazz, pop to blues.

It's a good idea for skaters to work with their coaches to select music. In the beginning, the coach usually chooses the music. Skaters' suggestions are always welcome, but skaters should listen to the wise advice of the coach, who is experienced in what the judges are looking for and what type of music is suitable for each skater's level and type of skating. Well known choreographer Sandra Bezic suggests considering the "age, style, physical structure, and especially the spirit of the skater." A petite seven-year-old should not be overpowered by a booming orchestration of Rachmaninoff. A delightful smile might lend itself to an Irish folk dance, while simple elegance might be underscored by new age music. The music must have an impact on both the skater, who should grow when selecting new music, and the audience. Perhaps a skater has never focused on a quiet flowing movement, a long spiral, or complicated footwork, but new music may inspire and focus these energies.

Listening to music can be very time-consuming. It is time spent at home when you could be doing a dozen other things. It can become very frustrating when you are pressured to find suitable music in a hurry. However, if you choose music away from the rink, at times when you are not under pressure to find something, it can become a pleasurable experience. There are two ways of doing this:

1. **Background music**—If you get in the habit of putting music on when you are at home, you can be reading or doing other things while the music is playing in the background. If there is music on the CD that is good for skating, your ears will probably perk up when you hear it. You can then stop what you are doing and write the selection in a notebook or card file for future use. If you listen to the radio, keep a note pad and pencil handy so that if you hear a good piece of music you can

Sections of this chapter have been reprinted with permission from the *PSA Coaches Manual*, 1999.

jot down the name. The next time you shop for music, you will have a particular selection to look for.

2. **Conscious listening**—After purchasing new CDs, you can sit down and consciously listen to the music, taking notes as you proceed. Use index cards and write down what you think of the CD in general, adding descriptive words about any selections you particularly like. You can file these cards by album number. Your index card may look something like this:

> #105 (Name of CD) Great music!
>
> Track 1: good beginning
>
> Track 4 (end): beautiful, slow
>
> Track 5: great ending
>
> Track 11: cute and bouncy
>
> Track 12 (middle): fast footwork

Often music will sound different in your living room than it will on the ice. Tiny details in the sound might be lost, and the music might sound soft and uneventful in the rink. When you listen to the music, envision the skating. Does the music bring to mind a spin, a huge jump, or intricate footwork?

When you put together two pieces of music, you should consider both the themes of the pieces and the tonal quality of the orchestrations or recordings. There should be a reason or story that explains why you put two pieces together. Do they come from the same musical? Are they both Spanish or from the same genre or era?

Another way of noting good music is to keep a card file for specific music moods or categories: dynamic, slow, fast footwork, low level, cute and bouncy, beginnings, endings—you name it. This is especially good if you are listening to music in the background and hear something you like. Just take an index card and write the CD number, track number, and a one-word thought about it, then file the card. When you're looking for a beautiful slow piece, you will be able to go to your card file and take out all of the cards under the heading *slow*. If you are looking for a fast footwork section, your card file will tell you exactly what you have.

Choreography

Once a piece of music has been picked, the skater should skate to the selection. Skating to the music is a good first step toward choreographing the program. An embarrassed fourteen year-old might shrug her shoulders and plead that she doesn't know what to do. Skaters should try to interpret the music and do what comes naturally. This process can generate ideas that you can later elaborate on, adding an arm movement or enhancing a step that was first done impromptu. Moving to the music gives the skater a feel for how to relate to the music. This exercise also involves them in the choreography.

Program Essentials

There are some basic things that can improve the choreography or style of any program: for example, eye focus, extension, pause and stop, high and low movements, good layout, and timing. Follow an arm with the eyes or intentionally focus the eyes elsewhere. In a spiral, on a jump landing, or in a simple connecting move, remember to point the toes, extend the arms and legs, and keep the head elevated.

Building a Music Library: Advice to Coaches

Before you shop for music, think about the kind of music you need. Consider the skater's ability, personality, age, size, strengths, weaknesses, and goals. With this in mind you have a more direct approach to shopping. If you don't have any need for music at this particular time, you can begin shopping for general categories of music. Later, when you need to find music, you will be able to choose from the selections you have collected.

Once you've organized your thoughts, you are ready to begin shopping:

- Find a music store with a large selection.
- Look for categories to fill your most immediate need.
- Check the specials (cut-outs and sales).
- Look for instrumentals.

You can become overwhelmed when you go into a music store to look for "good" skating music. Unless you know specific selections or composers, it's difficult to tell the difference between one CD and another. No matter how prepared you are, you still take a chance on the music. There will be times that you will buy a CD, only to get it home and find that there is nothing on it appropriate for skating. That is why it is a good idea to look for special sales, as you won't have invested so much if the CD was inexpensive. Most often, though, you will find at least one or two good selections on a CD, and sometimes it will be full of good music. Even if you don't find a usable piece, it might only be that you don't happen to have a student who is appropriate for the music at the present time. You might listen to the selection at some later date and find you have just the student for that particular music.

Different musical categories you might select from include:

Classical	Jazz
Overtures	Ethnic
Operettas	Disco
Musicals	Blues
Marches	Country
Waltzes	Folk
Ballets	Social
Polkas	Pop

Music Sources

CDs are slightly more expensive than cassettes but are far superior in quality and are much easier to edit. Many music stores provide listening stations so that you can sample music before purchasing. Libraries offer both CDs and cassettes on loan, although the selection is limited. Radio stations are a great listening source for both classical and popular music. Remember the conductor, the orchestra, and the arrangement of a particular piece of music. An arrangement of Scheherazade for violin and piano will be different from an arrangement performed by the Royal Philharmonic Orchestra.

Cataloging Your Music

To make it easy to find music when you want it, begin right away to catalog your collection. Think of categories for classifying your music so that you will have distinct sections that you can refer to when necessary. For example, you may want all classical music together or a separate section for ballets, as well as categories for jazz or disco and shows and musicals. However you do it, have a system that means something to you—you are the one who has to use it. Give each CD a number that indicates the category it belongs to. You might use 100s for classical, 200s for shows, and so on, or a letter/number combination (C for classical; S for shows). Put a little round sticker on the top left corner of each case to hold the CD number. You can use a different color sticker for each classification: yellow for classical, red for shows, and so on. Now that you have given each case a number, record all the CDs and their numbers in a notebook. Divide your notebook into the same sections as your cases and list each number and title in the appropriate section. When you are looking for music, you will be able to refer to your notebook, look over the lists, easily see what you want, and locate it in your collection by number.

Selecting Music for a Specific Skater

There are good and bad ways to go about selecting music for one of your skaters.

Selecting Music the Wrong Way

The following suggestions may make hunting for music fast and easy, but they are all unacceptable.

- Borrow a tape from another pro and record it for your student.
- Use any kind of music the student likes or brings in.
- Tell the parents to find something and cut it themselves.
- Give your student the same music Scott Hamilton used at the Olympics.
- Give this year's students copies of music you used for your students three years ago.
- Give seven-year-old Susie the music you used for your junior program.

If you're tempted to take the easy way, don't do it. The end result will probably be the wrong music for the skater in all the wrong ways. Anything worth doing is worth taking the time to do right.

Selecting Music the Right Way

Selecting music for your student is highly personal. It is not only important for performance value but also essential in the progress and development of the skater. The music should be there to challenge, excite, stimulate, and seduce. The selection should complement the skater's style yet be different enough to allow creativity. The slow skater can be encouraged to skate faster, the bouncy skater can learn to be more graceful, the shy skater can learn to add more spice to the program. If the music is chosen with great care, the skater will most certainly benefit. When listening to music for your student, you have three major things to think about: your student, the program, and the mood.

Consider the age, size (body build), level of skating, strength, personality, and natural style of your skater. If you have a tiny six-year-old, you don't want to give her heavy music. You might want to look for something with flutes or violins. If you have a girl who looks boyish or who skates like a football player charging down the field, you might want to soften her with a selection of graceful music to challenge her. As you listen to music, you will find that some types seem to definitely fit a male skater. Something that is bouncy and cute is perfect for a little girl. Something that is sophisticated might be for a teenager. All

(continued)

the while you must be thinking of the level of skating and the need to challenge, yet not overpower your skater.

Keeping Track of Recorded Music

Once you have recorded music, write down all the pertinent information in a notebook or card file. If you ever need to recut a tape or if in later years you want to use a certain cut again, you will have all the information at your fingertips. Your entry might look like this:

Program sample #1: Juvenile length

CD: West Side Story (Original Cast Recording) Track 10 Medley: "I Feel Pretty" 0:00–0:54

CD: West Side Story (Original Cast Recording) Track 10 Medley: "Maria" 0:55–1:32

CD: Broadway Favorites (Boston Pops) Track 8 Medley from West Side Story "America" 1:32–2:08

Program sample #2: Intermediate length

CD: Benjamin Britten: Young Persons Guide to the Orchestra "Matinees Musicales" London Symphony EMI records cdm 7 63777 2 Track 26 "Molto perpetuo" 0:00–1:06

CD: Benjamin Britten: Young Persons Guide to the Orchestra Track 34 "Tirolese" 1:06–1:39

CD: Benjamin Britten: Young Persons Guide to the Orchestra Track 26 "Moltoperpetuo" 1:39–2:33

Once you have finished putting together a tape, keep the original and make two copies for your student (one for practice and one for competition). You might also want to copy the original onto a master tape of all of your current music.

Today many coaches are using digital music editing. With the numerous software programs that are available and various effects that can enhance a cut, an almost seamless CD can be made by computer, stored, and catalogued for future use or editing.

If a sequence is intended to be short, choppy, and flexed, make that explicit too—but don't hover in a neutral zone. Take a beat or pause when it is appropriate. Hold that spiral a second longer, linger after a stop, or give emphasis to a landing position. Stillness can be as effective as movement. Use all the space around the body. Stretch high into the air above, and also create a movement near the ice. Combine the two by sweeping the ice and then reaching for the stars with extended arms.

Arranging the Elements

Think of all the required elements first. The music must be able to show off each element. There must be sufficient time for each element to be completed well. What is the required length of the program? How many mood changes do you need? Maybe it is a beginner program and you won't be cutting any other music with it. You need to think of this as you are listening to the music.

Always consider the pattern you are creating on the ice. Do the unexpected and turn outside the circle, do a rocker to change directions, or place a Lutz in the middle of the ice rather than in the corner. Order the difficult elements carefully. A skater who takes thirty seconds into the program to get settled should start with spins, spirals, or footwork. On the other hand, a skater who wants to get a jump out of the way and can consistently complete it should make it the opening move. Consider endurance: a death drop or a double Axel might be inconsistent and sloppy at the end of a program, yet dynamite in the opening.

Working With a Choreographer

A good choreographer should have a solid understanding of many different types of dance, including ballet, jazz, modern, social, ethnic, folk, country, and contemporary. The choreographer must know basic dance terminology and know the styles and works of the great dancers and choreographers. Knowledge of music, including the great composers as well as contemporary artists, is critical to the breadth and scope of the choreographer's creative abilities and the skater's ultimate success.

Applying this knowledge to skating can provide fresh, insightful, original works of creative programming that are challenging to the skater, enjoyable for the audience, and rewarded by the judges. Choreographers should never stop learning, growing, and experiencing all that the dance and musical world offer. By taking advantage of opportunities to go to a museum or attend a ballet, an opera, a jazz performance, or a group of flamenco dancers, choreographers can be richly inspired and motivated.

The coach, skater, and choreographer must be willing to laugh, cut loose, and be dramatic. Encourage exaggeration—a move might appear expressive from four feet away but might be lost when viewed from the top of the bleachers. Watch movement and dance outside the setting of the rink. Notice arm, head, and body movements in music videos, ballets, and shows.

When creating the program, the choreographer should keep the following variables in mind:

Student	Age
	Level of skating
	Body build
	Strength
	Personality
	Natural style
Program	Required elements
	Length of program
	Number of mood changes desired
Music	Beginning
	Slow part
	Footwork part
	Ending

The development of a program is an ongoing process. There is certainly a stage, as competition nears, where additions to the program are disruptive. On the other hand, it's important to keep the program growing. Experiment with an additional arm movement, a tilt of the head, or a combination jump.

Costuming

Costuming for a program must carry out the theme of the music. If you are doing an ethnic or period program, you should study and understand costuming for that

© Claus Andersen

Costuming should carry out the theme of the music.

culture or that era. If the music is soft and flowing, the costuming should be likewise. This principle is true for men as well as ladies. Brian Boitano accomplished this effect perfectly with flowing sleeves on his shirt when he skated in the 1988 Olympics to the music from the old silent movie *Napoleon*.

You also need to consider colors. If the music is loud and flashy, the costuming should reflect the same mood. If the music is hot and jazzy, red or black might be a good choice. Style and trim are individual choices. For the beginning skater, costumes are generally either homemade or purchased from a pro shop. Finding the right fit and style is similar to buying clothes in a department store. High-level and professional skaters can afford designers who can create skating outfit customized specifically for them.

Trim choices are optional. Test or competitive outfits are normally dressier than practice clothing, and often have elaborate trim. For performances some skaters prefer lots of sequins, rhinestones, and even feathers. Others, such as Michelle Kwan, favor a simpler look. Michelle always dresses very elegantly but tends to use a minimum of rhinestones, which enhances her sophisticated style and clean lines.

The important issue is always to ensure that the theme, music, and costume blend. Judges look for the complete package.

Summary

Music, choreography, and costuming are the bow that ties the whole skating package together. The package is not complete without good technical skating, but good skating without appropriate music, a creative program, and attractive costuming falls flat. Good coaches and choreographers pay close attention to these details and provide their skaters with a look that complements the program, pleases the audience, and attains high marks from the judges.

Scoring, Judges, and Performance Evaluation

Everyone who has performed in or watched a skating competition has at one time or another disagreed with the judges and wondered, "What in the world are they looking for? What were those judges thinking?" The answer lies in this simple statement: They are looking for the total package. Judges want to see good technique, artistry, presentation, appropriate costuming, good music, and a true love for skating that shines through during an exciting and charismatic performance. In other words, they want it all!

What Judges Look For

A good performance is technically and artistically sound, but a *great* performance has jumps that are a little higher and cleaner, spins that are faster and more centered, footwork that is dazzling, and a look that is polished. Most of the time, the great performance is obvious to all. The difficulty comes when small errors are made. Judges may disagree on which was the least serious of the errors or what tenth of a point should be awarded for something that was particularly well done.

In each element that is performed, judges look for specific qualities. In jumping, judges want to see difficulty, good height, control, clean landings, and consistency. Jumps are important but they are only part of the total package. Spins should be centered, fast, innovative, and controlled throughout all changes of position. Good spins should be rewarded, but the total program has less value if the spins are good but the jumps are poor. Good footwork is quick and rotates in both directions, demonstrates good edges, combines difficult turns, and covers the ice well. All elements should be spaced apart and choreographically balanced so that they are not placed in the same spot of the rink. The program should include variations in dynamics, fast and slow sections, and clockwise and counterclockwise movements.

Hair, costuming, and makeup also are an important part of the package. Each should match the theme of the program and make a cohesive statement about the skater and the performance.

The following are the rules for the scoring of *technical merit:*

- Difficulty of the performance
- Variety
- Cleanness and sureness
- Speed

In the scoring of *presentation,* the following are considered:

- Harmonious composition of the program as a whole and its conformity with the music chosen
- Variation of speed
- Utilization of the ice surface and space
- Easy movement and sureness in time to the music
- Carriage and style
- Originality
- Expression of the character of the music

Originality is one of the elements judges look for in a program. Here, Marina Anissina supports her partner, Gwendal Peizerat, in this innovative move.

Subjectivity of Skating

Sometimes a judge must choose between the elements of the packaging. Is the athletic ability more important than the artistry? What if the elements are beautifully executed but not very difficult? Most judges would say that a clean program is better than a difficult one that is poorly performed. Oftentimes, however, there are more gray areas than black and white. This is where the subjectivity in skating comes into play and where we see a divergence in the marking. When a judge has to make a decision between the elements of the packaging and determine which are more important, we see marks that have a wide range based primarily on individual preference. Just as two people may disagree on the beauty or integrity of a particular painting, judges may disagree on the quality of a skating performance. Judges also have personal preferences in skating styles. Some judges may prefer a lyrical style over an athletic style. There are certainly merits to each, but preferences will be reflected in the marking.

Summary

Skaters and coaches must realize that judges are hoping for a great performance. They want to see each skater do well. They are disappointed when a good skater has a bad day. Because they are placed in the position of judging a performance, they often get a bad rap for doing their job. Good judges encourage, support, and offer constructive advice to skaters about weaknesses in their programs.

Each skater must strive to do his or her very best in every practice and in every performance. Sometimes things do not go well. Those are the times when skaters and coaches learn the most. The main function of the judge is to evaluate the program and, in the process, elevate the skater's performance.

appendix Code of Ethics for Coaches

"As a coach, you are one of the most influential persons in a child's life. As a coach, you've got to help young people become all they were created to be. Your job is to produce good athletes, but more importantly, good people."

Jack Donohue, Coaches' Corner

Webster's New World Dictionary defines *ethics* as

"the system or code of morals of a particular group or profession; conforming to the standards of conduct of a given profession."

Defining ethical behavior for a skating professional is clear-cut in some instances and vague in others. Everyone knows that it is not ethical to steal another pro's students or to defame another coach. It is not ethical to approach parents and tell them that their pro is no good or that you could do a better job with their child. It is not ethical to give free lessons to the student of another pro. These are obvious examples.

A less obvious situation demanding ethical conduct may come up when you are not prepared. For example, suppose that Susie's mother just approached you and asked you for lessons. You have the time and you need the money, so why not accept right now? No more thought, of course. But wait! To be ethical you must first find out if Susie is taking lessons from another pro. Let's suppose she is! Now what do you do? The right thing is to handle the situation this way:

- Ask Susie's mother to notify the current pro of her decision to change to you.
- Contact the other pro to make sure he or she knows about the change.
- Once you have begun coaching Susie, avoid criticizing the methods taught by the previous coach. Be diplomatic in your approach, explaining that your methods are slightly different and that you need changes in order to build in your direction.

Remember, if a sticky situation occurs, don't just react; think first. If you are unsure how to handle the situation, seek advice from a more experienced pro. Being

---

The material in this appendix was provided by David Shulman, legal counsel for the Professional Skaters Association.

ethical is more than just a moral issue. No one wants to work in an environment where the air is constantly filled with tension. You are teaching a fun sport. You will certainly teach better in a relaxed and enjoyable atmosphere. This can only occur when the pros are kind to each other and ethical in their behavior. There is nothing worse than having to be constantly on your guard for fear of someone stealing your students. Be friendly, cooperative, and ethical; cultivate your own students, and your rewards will be far greater.

PSA Code of Ethics

1. Members of the Professional Skaters Association (hereafter referred to as *members*) shall at all times exercise the greatest care and discretion in their relationships with other members, pupils, and pupils of other members.

2. Prior to acting as coach to a skater, the member shall determine the nature and extent of any earlier teaching relationship between that skater and other members.

3. No member shall in any case solicit pupils of another member, directly or indirectly, or through third parties.

4. Members shall dress neatly and in a clean and appropriate manner as is becoming to a member of the Professional Skaters Association. Members shall be ever mindful of the influence they exercise over their pupils, and under all circumstances this trust should never be abused.

5. Members shall at all times be mindful that they have the responsibility to influence their students to act with dignity, ethics, and high moral conduct. Members shall never place the value of winning above the value of instilling the highest desirable ideas of character in their students, nor shall members act in any manner inconsistent with a high standard of ethical and moral conduct.

6. Members shall take an active role in the prevention of drug, alcohol, and tobacco abuse and under no circumstances should authorize the use of such products.

7. All members recognize that they shall act in a manner that avoids verbal or physical abuse of any skater, other coach, parent, or official. Members shall not engage in, nor shall members permit any skaters whom they are charged with the responsibility of coaching to engage in, any offense in violation of federal, state, or local law, or laws of a foreign government.

8. Members shall at all times avoid conflicts of interest, which can be considered to exist at any time when the actions of a member for his or herself or on behalf of a skater would involve the obtaining of an improper advantage.

Grievance Procedures

The PSA grievance procedure is an important function of the association. It is of primary importance to the public and to the members of the PSA that cases involving claims of unethical conduct filed against a member of the PSA receive prompt investigation and are reviewed with fairness and justice.

To file a grievance, you must send a signed, notarized letter stating the reason for the grievance along with documentation and evidence to the grievance committee chairman. There is a filing fee. A copy of your letter is then sent to the person against whom the grievance has been filed. That person must respond with a signed, notarized letter, a copy of which is sent to you. These procedures are repeated twice.

If further action needs to be taken, the grievance committee, composed of members appointed by the president, reviews the case and determines the next steps. If disciplinary action is required, a five step process is followed:

1. Private admonition
2. Public admonition
3. Probation
4. Suspension
5. Expulsion

Once action has been determined, a letter is sent to the person who has been cited explaining the length of time, rights, privileges, and monitoring of the specific action taken against him or her. A notification of the action taken is also sent to the person who filed the grievance.

In many ways, each member of the PSA represents every other member of the PSA each time a member teaches, speaks, or otherwise comes into contact with the public. Each member should strive to be competent, be diligent, and demonstrate integrity. The PSA rules on grievance procedures are designed to encourage integrity and give guidance to persons claiming breach of ethics.

Tenets of Professionalism

The purpose of these tenets is to provide a framework of conduct above and beyond the minimum standards provided by the code of ethics as set forth in the PSA bylaws.

The PSA is aware that applicable rules of ethics covering professional responsibility generally provide only minimum standards of acceptable conduct. The PSA and its membership aspire to the highest ideals of professionalism and acknowledge that members should follow the following tenets of conduct when providing professional services:

1.   As coaches of skating, PSA members will conduct themselves in a manner that demonstrates respect for the rules under which skaters compete, and they will preserve the decorum and integrity of the testing program and competition.

2.   The Professional Skaters Association recognizes that professional courtesy is consistent with the role of the coach. Members of the PSA will be civil and courteous to all with whom they come in contact and will endeavor to maintain a collegial relationship with other coaches.

3.   As skating coaches, members acknowledge that from time to time the students with whom they work may wish to leave a coach and seek coaching elsewhere. Members acknowledge that they will cooperate with other coaches when conflicts arise and will be willing to make such changes on behalf of the students as will complement the further performance and progress of each student.

4.   When competitions or testing situations arise, members agree to keep their students and the parents of those students well informed and to involve them in making decisions that affect their interest. At the same time, members agree to avoid emotional attachment to students and their activities both in skating and out of skating which might impair the members' ability to render professional service.

5.   As professionals, PSA members will honor their promises and commitments, whether oral or in writing, and will strive to build a reputation for dignity, honesty, and integrity in the skating profession.

6.   Members will not make groundless accusations of impropriety or attribute bad motives to other coaches in bad faith or without good cause.

7.   Members will not engage in any course of conduct designed to harass another coach, skating organization official, skater, or parent of another skater.

8.   Members will strive to expand their knowledge of skating and to achieve and maintain proficiency in this area of expertise.

9.   PSA members will never allow race, gender, religion, age, or other suspect classifications of persons to improperly motivate their actions.

10.   At all times and in all things when dealing with the skating public, officials, and other members of the coaching profession, members will adhere to the proposition that all practices shall be governed by the principals of honesty and integrity.

Ratings

Ratings are available only to PSA full members in good standing who have attended at least one workshop, seminar, conference PEP (Professional Education Program), or PACE (Professional Accreditation and Certification Education) program prior to applying for a rating.

Rated professionals, including those who have passed the written exam, must obtain a total of 24 education credits every three years in order to maintain a rating. Coaches who do not actively maintain their education credits or current membership have an inactive rating. An inactive rating will be listed in the PSA directory. Coaches may not advertise their ratings unless they are active.

All rating panels consist of three master coaches. When necessary, a senior rated coach may serve as a minority panel member. There may be one trial examiner present.

Ratings are offered for free skating, figures, dance, pairs, group, program administration, synchronized team, choreography and style, and moves in the field.

For further information contact the PSA office by phone (507-281-5122), fax (507-281-5491), or e-mail (**office@skatepsa.com**).

glossary

apex—The pinnacle or point where maximum height is achieved in a jump.

axis—An imaginary straight line that a skater rotates around on a spin or jump. It is also the line that runs lengthwise through a figure or a pattern.

check—To stop or control rotation by reversing the arms against the hips.

free foot—The foot that is free from the ice, enabling all the body weight to be distributed over the skating side.

jump combination—Links two jumps together by using the landing foot of the first jump as the takeoff for the second jump.

jump sequence—Three or more jumps linked together.

over the skating hip—The skater is balanced on one foot, moving either forward or backward, and the hips are aligned in perfect balance with the shoulder and skating foot.

print—The line left on the ice by the blade of the skating foot. Synonymous with *tracing.*

rink barrier—The hockey boards that surround the circumference of the rink.

scissor action—A movement of the free foot opposite to the direction in which the skating foot is moving, followed by another movement once again in the opposite direction.

skating foot—The foot that is on the ice bearing the weight of the body.

square—Hips and shoulders lined up with each other and horizontal to the line of the print.

tracing—The line left on the ice by the blade of the skating foot. Synonymous with *print.*

traveling—Instead of being centered on one spot during a spin, the skater moves, or "travels," across the ice, leaving a print of loop circles rather than one concentric circle.

index

About the Professional Skaters Association

The Professional Skaters Association (PSA) is the oldest and largest professional skaters' association in the world. Formed in 1938, the association focuses primarily on education and accreditation. Its headquarters are in Rochester, Minnesota.

Coaches who take their profession seriously join the Professional Skaters Association to obtain accreditation and education. They regularly attend coaching seminars to update their skills, advance their knowledge, and network with other coaches from around the world. To obtain information, contact the office by phone at 507-281-5122 or by e-mail at **office@skatepsa.com**.

about the author

A former competitive skater and a master PSA instructor, Carole Shulman is presently the executive director of the Professional Skaters Association (PSA) and the editor of *The Professional Skater* magazine. She has also served as a professional figure skating judge.

As an amateur competitor Shulman won gold medals in figures, freestyle, and pairs from the U.S. Figure Skating Association. She holds a master rating in figure skating, freestyle, pairs, and group skating as well as in program administration and choreography. She is a master examiner for PSA accreditation exams.

Shulman lives in Rochester, Minnesota, with her husband, David. Her favorite leisure activities are downhill skiing, boating, and ballroom dancing.

You'll find
other outstanding
sport resources at

www.humankinetics.com

In the U.S. call

1-800-747-4457

Australia 08 8277 1555
Canada 1-800-465-7301
Europe .... +44 (0) 113 278 1708
New Zealand 09-523-3462

HUMAN KINETICS
The Premier Publisher for Sports & Fitness
P.O. Box 5076 • Champaign, IL 61825-5076 USA